W9-AVC-611

THE NEXT SUPERPOWER

Other books by Mark Finley:

2000 and Beyond

Angel Wars

Confidence Amid Chaos

Dark Tunnels and Bright Lights

Discover Jesus

Experiencing God

Final Days

God's Last Altar Call

Greater Expectations

Growing Through Life's Toughest Times

Hearts at Home

Hope for a New Century

Jerusalem Showdown

Jesus Face to Face

Lonely No Longer

Looking for God in All the Wrong Places

More Seeing Is Believing

A Promise a Day

Questioning the Supernatural

A Religion That Works

Revelation Predictions

Revelation's Three Greatest Mysteries

Search for Certainty Bible Study Guides

Simply Salvation

Soul Care

The Stress Transformers

Strong Medicine for a Sick Society

Studying Together

They're Coming Home

Things That Matter Most

Thirteen Life-changing Secrets

The Thought Makers

To Hope Again

Unshakable Faith

What Happy Couples Know

What My Parents Did Right

What You Can Know for Sure

When Faith Crumbles

When Your Faith Is Shaken

Which Way America?

THE NEXT SUPERPOWER

Ancient Prophecies, Global Events, and Your Future

MARK FINLEY

REVIEW AND HERALD® PUBLISHING ASSOCIATION
HAGERSTOWN, MD 21740

The Review and Herald Publishing Association publishes biblically based materials for spiritual, physical, and mental growth and Christian discipleship.

This book was
Edited by Gerald Wheeler
Copyedited by Richard Coffen
Designed by Trent Truman
Cover photo by Getty Images
Typeset: Goudy 11/15

PRINTED IN U.S.A.
09 08 07 06 5 4 3 2

R&H Cataloging Service
Finley, Mark A., 1945- .
The next superpower.

1. Bible—Prophecies. I. Title.

236.

ISBN-10: 0-8280-1918-5
ISBN-13: 978-0-8280-1918-7

CONTENTS

ACKNOWLEDGMENTS

I pay tribute to a corps of special people who have made this project possible: Ken McFarland edited some of my original lectures; Dan Houghton, of Hart Research, graciously granted permission for me to use material published in some of my earlier works; Gerald Wheeler did a masterful editorial job; and my wife, Ernestine, encouraged me to place priority on this all-important project. I would also like to thank Mr. and Mrs. Martin Butler for countless hours spent typing the manuscript. Most of all, I give glory to God for His Word, upon which these words are based.

MARK FINLEY

INTRODUCTION

Whenever they hear the word "prophecy," many think of the garish tabloids they see at the checkout counter, telling of global wars and plagues, meteorite crashes, stock market collapses, and endless other disasters. Some of the prophecies they feature appear to be based on parts of the Bible. But such sensationalistic predictions make thinking people suspicious of the whole concept of prophecy. In the religious world, popular novels and movies present other forms of prophecy that claim to be more biblically based. But are they any more reliable than the supermarket tabloids?

The Bible really has much to say about the future. Unfortunately, religious people do not seem to agree on what it means. The fact that they interpret biblical prophecy in sometimes radically opposite ways causes others to wonder if we can understand Scripture at all. If Bible prophecy is important, why did God make it sometimes so difficult to understand? What is the key to unlocking biblical prophecy? Have any of the Bible's prophecies actually been fulfilled? Or are they meaningless ancient writings?

Mark Finley, who has studied and lectured on the Bible for most of his life, believes that we can understand biblical prophecy—if we let Scripture explain itself. The Bible frequently presents its views of the future in special symbolic language—but then carefully defines those symbols. Finley first takes us step by step through ancient prophecies that have already come to pass. Once he has established the way Bible writers have presented past prophecies and demonstrated their reliability and accuracy, he guides us through prophecies whose fulfillment is yet future. Also he explains the important biblical teachings behind those future events.

Today we live in a chaotic and frightening world. Many see prophecy as warning only of more terrible events. But biblical prophecy actually holds out hope. It foretells of a superpower that will inaugurate a world in which death and disaster, sorrow and suffering, and tears and turmoil will vanish forever. Prophecy brings us not fear but joy. It brings us hope guaranteed by an all-powerful God.

THE PUBLISHERS

CHAPTER 1

SECRETS OF ANCIENT SCROLLS

Self-proclaimed prophets proudly predict tomorrow's headlines with confidence. They claim to know world events in advance. Somehow, they declare, they have a direct line to the Almighty or the forces that rule the universe.

Such pundits warn of the imminent collapse of the stock market, dramatic changes in weather patterns, international famines, massive tsunamis, devastating diseases, nuclear destruction, or the coming catastrophic collapse of civilization.

As a new millennium dawned some years ago, doomsday predictions increased dramatically. More than 250 Web sites currently present end-time scenarios. One of the most popular prognosticators with a following of millions has been Nostradamus. The sixteenth-century French psychic claimed to be able to forecast the future by sitting atop a brass tripod. Nostradamus made hundreds of predictions. A modern interpretation of one of his most famous prophecies stated that in early 1999 or 2000 "clashes among racial, ethnic, and nationalist groups in Eastern Europe climax with the use of nuclear weapons. Millions are not only feared dead—they are dead. What used to be considered European 'civilization' is an increasingly distant memory."

Obviously, the prophecy utterly failed. It just didn't happen. The same applies to scores of other purported predictions of the end. Here is an interpretation of a prophecy by Edgar Cayce, the "Sleeping Prophet," who died in 1945: "There will be a major financial crash in January of 2000.

SIEGFRIED HORN MUSEUM

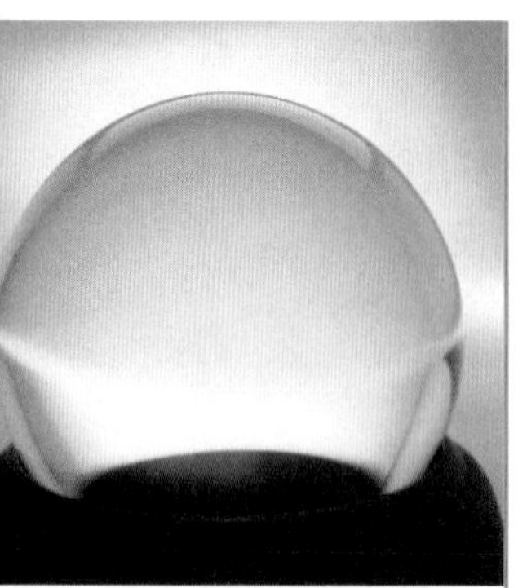

HUMAN BEINGS CANNOT ACCURATELY FORETELL THE FUTURE. ONLY GOD HIMSELF CAN TELL WHAT WILL HAPPEN BEFOREHAND.

Vicious ice and electrical storms will rake the United States and Western Europe, killing a million or more senior citizens and other innocent people who lost their homes or incomes in the January crash."

His forecast of the future was way off the mark. In addition to these doomsday prophets predicting the world's tragic end, we find a growing number of would-be "messiahs" who claim they can save the world from annihilation. In November of 1970 a 12-year-old Indian guru named Maharaj Ji made this pledge: "I declare I will establish peace in this world." In three years he formed a massive worldwide organization dedicated to ending war and suffering in the world. Maharaj Ji spoke to large audiences in such huge stadiums as the Houston Astrodome in Texas. As hundreds of thousands bowed to the "perfect living master," four associates carried the guru onto the stage as he sat on a golden satin pillow in a golden chair. More than 30 years later peace still has not come. The world is riddled with war, racked by strife, gripped with famine, and torn apart by conflict. Amazingly enough, in the past 50 years more than 1,100 religious leaders throughout the world have claimed to be Christ or the world's savior to usher in "the new age" or a millennium of peace.

In an English village in 1792 an illiterate domestic servant named Joanna Southcott became mentally unbalanced. Shortly she journeyed to London, where she developed a following called Southcottians. Remnants of this small sect still exist today. The woman made a small fortune from the sale of her prophecies and certificates guaranteeing her followers salvation. She predicted in 1814 that as the bride of Christ she would give birth to Shiloh on October 19, 1814. Nothing happened, and she died of a brain disease on December 27, 1814.

She left behind a sealed box with instructions that it not be opened until humanity needed its contents to solve some great world crisis. The

PHOTODISC

box remained shut for more than a century. Someone allegedly opened it in 1927. It simply contained a novel, a lottery ticket, a dice box, a puzzle, a woman's nightcap, and a pistol. The sealed contents meant absolutely nothing. Joanna's followers longed for some message of hope regarding the future, but they were bitterly disappointed.

Tragically, such so-called prophets and messiahs have left millions of their followers in confusion. Is there anyone who can predict the future with accuracy? Where can we find hope for tomorrow? Is there any reliable source of information regarding the future? Are there sealed contents in some long-neglected box that will enable us to face the future with greater confidence? Could it even be possible that this box is sitting on the shelf in your very home?

Although often overlooked, neglected, criticized, condemned, and ostracized by some people, the Bible has proved itself reliable down through the centuries. Its predictions have unfolded for more than 2,500 years. Unfortunately many dismiss the Bible's claims. Their prejudice keeps them from intelligently considering it. I am confident that you are open-minded enough to carefully consider the evidence and make your own decision regarding the Bible's prophetic accuracy and truthfulness. One of the great advantages we have in our search for truth and our study of Scripture has been the passing of the centuries. Let me explain. More than 40 authors wrote the Bible over a 1,600-year span. Moses wrote the first book of the Bible, Genesis, in approximately 1500 B.C. John composed the last book, Revelation, toward the end of the first century. The 66 books of the Bible contain numerous predictions. Those predictions deal with the rise and fall of empires; the demise of rulers; the destruction of cities; the birth, life, death, and resurrection of the Messiah; the fate of the nation of Israel; end-time events; and the return of our Lord.

THE BIBLE HAS PROVED ITSELF RELIABLE DOWN THROUGH THE CENTURIES.

If prophecies in the past have already been fulfilled, we can have a rea-

EVIDENCES OF THE BIBLE'S INSPIRATION

1	**COHESIVE UNITY:** Although more than 40 authors of varied background wrote the Bible during a 1,600-year period of time, it has unity on all points of faith, giving evidence of a divine mind guiding the minds of each human writer.
2	**INTERNAL DECLARATION:** The Bible declares it is inspired. In more than 3,000 places it claims to be the word of God. It either is what it says, or it is a book of fabrications. How could a book with such high moral claims possibly be a book of lies?
3	**FULFILLED PROPHECY:** Hundreds of specific prophecies have been fulfilled. These prophecies reveal events in the history of Israel, the rise and fall of nations, and the life of Jesus.
4	**LIFE-CHANGING POWER:** Millions testify to the Bible's life-changing power. For those who open its pages with an inquiring mind, the book speaks with incredible power.
5	**PERENNIAL APPEAL:** For years the Bible has been the world's best seller.
6	**UNIVERSAL APPEAL:** The Bible appeals to young and old, rich and poor, educated and uneducated. Parts of the Bible have been translated into more than 1,000 of the world's languages, and millions of copies continue to be printed each year.

sonable amount of confidence that the Bible's prophecies regarding the future will also come to pass. Fulfilled prophecy gives us confidence that what God has declared about the future He will also make happen. One of the clearest evidences of the Bible's inspiration is its ability to foretell future events. Such fulfilled Bible prophecy verifies the truthfulness of God's Word. God does not guess—He knows and makes happen (Isaiah 14:24, 27; Isaiah 40:22, 23; Isaiah 44:24-26) .

God separates Himself from all false deities, pretend prophets, and so-called messiahs by challenging them with these words: "Remember the former things, those of long ago; I am God, and there is no other; I am God, and there is none like me. I make known the end from the beginning, from ancient times, what is still to come" (Isaiah 46:9, 10).

There is no one else in the universe like Him. Why? The Lord has the ability to foretell the future. With God the future is always present. He knows tomorrow better than we know this moment. And God has revealed Himself to His prophets in visions, dreams, and through the direct inspiration of His Spirit. The apostle Paul declares that "all scripture is given by inspiration of God" (2 Timothy 3:16, KJV). Peter adds that "men spoke from God as they were carried along by the Holy Spirit" (2 Peter 1:21). The Bible is God's revelation to humanity. Its prophecies help establish its credibility. They attest to the Lord's ability to reveal future events before they happen.

FULFILLED PROPHECY

Let's consider some of these amazing Bible predictions. For example, the Egyptians dominated the world scene for centuries. The mighty empire of the pharaohs with its fabulous treasures has captured imaginations. Lavish palaces, massive pyramids, and amazing cities sprang from the desert sands. The world-famous pyramids at Giza are one of the wonders of ancient civilization. The Great Pyramid of Cheops towers more than 450 feet above the desert floor (that's a whopping 48 stories high) and sprawls over 13 acres. The massive monument consists of 2.3 million blocks of stone, weighing 1.5 to 3 tons each. Archaeologists estimate that it took 120,000 workers more than 20 years to build the Great Pyramid.

EGYPT'S FUTURE FORECAST

In its day Egypt appeared invincible. Its army was superior to any in the world, and its wealth was unparalleled. For many centuries the city of Memphis was the capital of this mighty nation. The Egyptians believed their gods provided them with their source of power. But during the seventh century B.C. the biblical prophet Ezekiel made a series of incredible predictions regarding Egypt. He declared, "This is what the Sovereign

PHOTODISC

Lord says: I will destroy the idols and put an end to the images in Memphis. No longer will there be a prince in Egypt, and I will spread fear throughout the land" (Ezekiel 30:13). "So I will inflict punishment on Egypt, and they will know that I am the Lord" (verse 19). "I am against Pharaoh king of Egypt. . . . I will disperse the Egyptians among the nations and scatter them through the countries" (verses 22, 23).

"For this is what the Sovereign Lord says: The sword of the king of Babylon will come against you. I will cause your hordes to fall by the swords of mighty men. . . . They will shatter the pride of Egypt, and all her hordes will be overthrown" (Ezekiel 32:11, 12).

Just as the prophet predicted, the Babylonians attacked Egypt and overthrew the mighty empire. The invaders took some of its people captive and scattered them across Mesopotamia. In addition, through the centuries grave robbers have plundered the treasures of Egypt's palaces, tombs, and pyramids. Other in-

THE WORLD-FAMOUS PYRAMIDS AT GIZA ARE ONE OF THE SEVEN WONDERS OF ANCIENT CIVILIZATION.

vaders have smashed the idols of Memphis. Today the once-mighty city, boastful in its arrogance, lies in ruins. By the nineteenth century Egyptologist Amelia Edwards could comment, "And this is all that remains of Memphis, oldest of cities: a few rubbish heaps—a dozen or so broken statues and a name. . . . Where are the stately ruins which even in the Middle Ages extended over the space of half-a-day's journey in each direction? One can hardly believe that a great city flourished on this spot or understand how it should have been effaced so utterly" (*A Thousand Miles Up the Nile*, pp. 97-99).

The magnificent ancient Egyptian civilization today survives only as crumbling and sand-covered ruins.

She made a fascinating point when she pointed out that one can "hardly believe" or "understand" how Egypt's capital Memphis could be so utterly destroyed. When we look through the eyes of Bible prophecies, though, the explanation is clear. God does not guess—He knows, because through His power He makes them come to pass.

THE DESTRUCTION OF TYRE

Egypt was not the only victim of Babylon's wrath. Nebuchadnezzar, the empire-building Babylonian king, also turned his attention on Tyre—a seaport city in the region of what is now modern-day Lebanon. Tyre was the mistress of the Mediterranean Sea and a commercial center. Carthage, which would later be the rival of Rome, began as a colony of Tyre. This thriving complex of cities stretched 20 miles along the eastern shores of the Mediterranean Sea. Incredibly, seven miles of that distance was especially densely populated. Ships from all nations anchored in its harbor. Wealthy merchants bartered in its streets. Again, Ezekiel, a bib-

Gerald Wheeler

lical prophet, burst upon the scene with these amazing predictions: "This is what the Sovereign Lord says: I am against you, O Tyre, and I will bring many nations against you, like the sea casting up its waves. They will destroy the walls of Tyre and pull down her towers; I will scrape away her rubble and make her a bare rock. Out in the sea she will become a place to spread fishnets, for I have spoken. . . . She will become plunder for the nations" (Ezekiel 26:3-5).

The prophet adds even more details. The preciseness of prophecies in the Bible help to confirm the book's authenticity. The minute details reveal the impossibility of human wisdom making some general observation regarding the future. Note carefully Ezekiel's prophetic insights.

Today, as Ezekiel predicted long ago, the site of Tyre is still a place for fishers to dry and mend their nets.

"They will plunder your wealth and loot your merchandise; they will break down your walls and demolish your fine houses and throw your stones, timber and rubble into the sea. . . . I will make you a bare rock, and you will become a place to spread fish-

Ken Vine

nets. You will never be rebuilt, for I the Lord have spoken" (verses 12-14). Notice at least four major aspects of the prophecy. First, Tyre would be utterly destroyed. Second, its site would be scraped bare like the top of a rock and left as a place for the spreading of fishing nets. Third, its destroyers would dump its ruins into the sea. And last of all, no one would ever rebuild the once-proud city.

PROPHECY DECLARED THAT THE SITE OF THE CITY OF TYRE WOULD BE SCRAPED DOWN TO THE BARE ROCK AND WOULD NOT BE REBUILT.

Events precisely fulfilled the prophecy. Every detail came to pass. Nebuchadnezzar, the Babylonian king, viciously attacked Tyre. Even then it took 13 years to destroy the land part of the city. Its ruins lay along the Mediterranean Sea for two and a half centuries. The final detail of the prophecy took place when Alexander the Great literally scraped the land part of Tyre bare like a rock. He dumped the rubble from its ancient ruins into the sea to build a causeway a half mile long to attack the part of Tyre surrounded by water. Today Tyre is indeed a place where fishers spread their nets.

The city has never been rebuilt to its former greatness. Throughout history many cities have undergone destruction and most have been rebuilt. The ravages of war decimated such cities as Rome, Italy; Frankfurt, Germany; London, England; Hiroshima, Japan; and a host of others. Today they are again thriving metropolises. But Tyre is not.

ANCIENT PETRA SPEAKS OF FULFILLED PROPHECY

A number of years ago I was deeply impressed with the accuracy of Bible prophecy when I visited the ruins of the city of Petra in modern Jordan. Petra was the ancient capital of the Edomites. Our It Is Written television crew entered the city through the Siq, or cleft in the rock, KEN VINE

Siegfried Horn Museum

The incredible city of Petra, carved out of the solid rock as the capital of the Edomites, now lies desolate.

more than a mile long. The setting is magnificent. Through the centuries the city's inhabitants carved 3,000 structures from the red limestone cliffs. They include palaces, government offices, theaters, temples, and, most of all, tombs, all carefully chiseled out of the multicolored stone. As I wandered around among the empty tombs and stared at the lifeless ruins, I thought about the thriving civilization that had once existed there. For centuries the city has lain desolate. No one lives there today. Its streets are barren, its shops and its once-luxurious facades crumbling in the blazing Jordanian desert sun.

As the sun set over the carved edifices of Petra, painting the city in a purplish hue, I recalled Isaiah's words about the destruction that would strike Edom, the site of Petra: "From generation to generation it will lie desolate" (Isaiah 34:10). The words of the prophet come echoing down through the centuries. Resounding off the cliffs of Edom, they speak to all generations. "The grass withers and the flowers fall, but the word of our God stands" (Isaiah 40:8). The Word of God is eternally true. Its reliability passes the test of the centuries. The secrets of the ancient scrolls speak to us in the twenty-first century. While there are not many things you can count on in life, one thing is always certain—God's Word is trustworthy.

But the Bible is more than a book of prophecy. Millions testify to the dramatic changes in their lives as they have read its pages. The apostle James counsels us to "humbly accept the word planted in you, which can save you" (James 1:21). The same Holy Spirit who inspired the writers of the Bible also guides those who read it. The Bible is not an ordinary book. Some books are inspiring—the Bible is inspired. Some books may be enlightening—the Bible comes from "the light of the world" (John 8:12). Some books contain fragments of eternal truth—the Bible is the essence of truth (John 17:17). And while some books influence your thinking, the Bible changes your life.

In early 2000 a criminal group landed a helicopter on the roof of the National Bank in Port Moresby, Papua New Guinea, determined to pull off the robbery of the century. Brandishing their AK-47 assault rifles, they burst into the bank and demanded the bank tellers turn over all their cash. The director of the bank barricaded himself in his office and called an emergency hotline tied directly into the nation's presidential security group. It immediately dispatched a team of special forces. In the resulting gunfight all but one of the robbers died. The authorities imprisoned him.

SOME BOOKS CONTAIN FRAGMENTS OF ETERNAL TRUTH—THE BIBLE IS THE ESSENCE OF TRUTH.

When I held a series of gospel meetings on the power of Jesus and His Word in Port Moresby's Sir John Guise Stadium, this criminal, now out of prison, attended. God had worked a miracle in his life. The Holy Spirit had touched his heart and transformed him. He had experienced grace, mercy, forgiveness, and God's life-changing power. Today he rejoices in his newfound faith. What God did for this man, He will do for you. As you read this book, ask God to work a miracle in your life, too!

CHAPTER 2

SUPER LEADER

Prof. James Strange of the University of South Florida in the United States was fascinated with the specific prophecies of Christ's birth, life, death, and resurrection. The professor developed a complex mathematical formula to discover the statistical probability of all these incredibly amazing prophecies being fulfilled. His conclusion: the chances were 1 in 1 billion to the sixteenth power—that is 1 with a whopping 144 zeros after it.

Jesus Himself used the evidence of fulfilled Bible prophecy to demonstrate that He was the world's true Messiah. Shortly after His resurrection He met two of His disciples on the Emmaus road. Deeply distressed over the events of the past few days, they felt confused and perplexed. Because the Holy Spirit blinded them, they did not immediately recognize Jesus. During the journey "he said to them, 'How foolish you are, and how slow of heart to believe all that the prophets have spoken! Did not the Christ have to suffer these things and then enter his glory?'" (Luke 24:25, 26). Jesus clearly pointed out that the recent events, which had so confused their minds, were actually a fulfillment of prophecy.

The Savior then shared amazing insights from the Word of God that left no doubt of His identity. He unfolded who He was from the prophecies of the Old Testament. "And beginning with Moses and all the Prophets, he explained to them what was said in all the Scriptures concerning himself" (verse 27).

Wouldn't it have been thrilling if someone could have recorded Jesus' discussion with the two disciples and we could play it back today? Although we were not there, we do have a pretty good idea of what Jesus said. He began with the first five books of the Bible—Genesis, Exodus, Leviticus, Numbers, and Deuteronomy—and continued through the rest of the Old Testament, pinpointing with uncanny accuracy the predictions of the Old Testament prophets that His life had fulfilled.

A LIFE WRITTEN BEFOREHAND

Most biographies get written at the end of a person's life. Aspects of Jesus' life were written before He was born. His life fulfilled prophecies centuries old. Millennia before His birth the human race looked forward to the coming of the Messiah. Some 1,500 years before Christ's birth Moses wrote of the Messiah, who would "bruise" the serpent's head and also have His heel bruised (Genesis 3:15, KJV). Every sacrificial lamb offered by Old Testament believers gave a vivid testimony that they believed the Messiah would come to deal a crushing blow to the evil one. The prophet Isaiah reveals that "the Lord himself will give you a sign: The virgin will be with child and will give birth to a son, and will call him Immanuel" (Isaiah 7:14). The name Immanuel means "God [is] with us." The virgin birth is one of Christianity's central truths. The Holy Spirit supernaturally conceived Jesus in the womb of Mary. The angel Gabriel appeared to her, declaring, "Do not be afraid, Mary, you have found favor with God. You will be with child and give birth to a son, and you are to give him the name Jesus" (Luke 1:30, 31). The same angelic being also visited her future husband, Joseph, quoting Isaiah's prophecy regarding the Messiah being born of a virgin: "Do not be afraid to take Mary home as your wife, because what is conceived in her is from the Holy Spirit" (Matthew 1:20).

> **THE LIFE OF JESUS FULLFILLED PROPHECIES GIVEN CENTURIES BEFORE.**

Jesus was more than a good man, a religious teacher, or even an ethical philosopher. He was the divine Son of God conceived supernaturally

HOW THE DIVINE SON OF GOD CAN TRANSFORM YOUR LIFE

1	When God created humanity, He established it perfect without a taint of sin or rebellion (Genesis 1:26, 27).
2	As the result of their conscious choice Adam and Eve sinned. Sin separates us from God (Isaiah 59:2).
3	The wages of sin is death (Romans 6:23).
4	All humankind have sinned (Romans 3:23). Consequently we all deserve death.
5	In His love and mercy God graciously offers us the gift of eternal life (Ephesians 2:8).
6	Jesus lived the life we should have lived and died the death we should have died (John 3:16; Romans 5:12-19).
7	To accept Jesus means that we acknowledge that we cannot save ourselves. Openly admitting that we are lost sinners, we accept His death as atonement for our sins (John 1:17).
8	By accepting Christ, we receive His gift of eternal life (1 John 5:11, 12).

in Mary's womb by the Holy Spirit. Wonder of all wonders, Isaiah predicted the virgin birth more than six centuries in advance.

DETAILS REGARDING JESUS' BIRTH REVEALED

The prophet Micah adds this significant detail: "But you, Bethlehem Ephrathah, though you are small among the clans of Judah, out of you will come for me one who will be ruler over Israel, whose origins are from of old, from ancient times" (Micah 5:2). Most people are aware that Jesus' hometown was Nazareth. Bethlehem is about 70 miles south. In the days of Jesus it was an extremely small village—truly "small among the clans of Judah." How did Micah the prophet predict centuries before that Mary would arrive in the city the very night of Jesus' birth? Under normal circumstances women don't take 70-mile donkey rides when they are ready to deliver a child. It was a decree of Caesar Augustus that brought the holy family to Bethlehem. Quirinius (Cyrenius), governor of Syria, ordered the census for tax purposes. It required families to leave their homes and return to the city of their birth. How did the ancient prophet know that Bethlehem would be the birthplace of the Messiah? Bible prophets do not guess—they are inspired by the living God.

In one of the oldest messianic prophecies ever recorded, the prophet Balaam declared, "A star will come out of Jacob; a scepter will rise out of Israel" (Numbers 24:17). Magi from the East noted a new star in the night sky, one that marked Christ's arrival. They traveled to Jerusalem, expecting the entire city to be buzzing with talk about the nation's Messiah. Surely all Israel would be excited about its new ruler. But instead, the Magi were stunned at the lack of enthusiasm about the birth of the Messiah. When Herod learned of their presence in Jerusalem, he sent for them and inquired what time the star had appeared. Then he dispatched them on their way, telling them to bring word to him when they found the Messiah so that he could worship Him as well. The Gospel writer Matthew records the story of the Magi following the star, which led them directly to the newborn babe in Bethlehem. God forewarned the Magi in a dream not to report back to Herod (Matthew 2:1-12).

JACOB'S PATRIARCHAL BLESSING FORETELLS THE MESSIAH

When the dying Jacob gathered his sons together for the patriarchal blessing, he encouraged Judah with these words: "The sceptre shall not depart from Judah, nor a lawgiver from between his feet, until Shiloh come" (Genesis 49:10, KJV). Many believe that Shiloh is another name for the Messiah. It probably means the one who brings peace. Jesus is the great peacemaker. He brings peace, reconciliation, forgiveness, grace, and mercy.

Jacob's prediction spells out clearly that Judah would be the ruling tribe at the time of the Messiah's birth. Events exactly fulfilled his prediction. The patriarch had 12 sons, so the odds of the old man guessing right were about 1 in 12. I am not a betting man, but if I were, I wouldn't like 12 to 1 odds. And the odds of Jesus' being born in Bethlehem were even greater. They were at least 1,000 to 1. I wouldn't take those odds anytime, and neither would you.

JESUS' MINISTRY REVEALED

God specifically gave the prophecies detailing aspects of Christ's life in advance to reveal who Jesus really is. They are not meant simply to satisfy our intellectual curiosity. In one of the most extensive prophecies of the Bible, Isaiah outlines parts of Jesus' ministry in advance. The prophet states, "The Spirit of the Sovereign Lord is on me, because the Lord has anointed me to preach good news to the poor. He has sent me to bind up the brokenhearted, to proclaim freedom for the captives and release from darkness for the prisoners, to proclaim the year of the Lord's favor and . . . to comfort all who mourn" (Isaiah 61:1, 2).

Isaiah declared that the Messiah would come "to bind up the brokenhearted, to proclaim freedom for the captives."

Siegfried Horn Museum/Nathan Greene

SIEGFRIED HORN MUSEUM/NATHAN GREENE

AS THE PROPHET WROTE LONG AGO, JESUS PREACHED "GOOD NEWS TO THE POOR" AND GAVE THEM HOPE AND THE PROMISE OF ETERNAL LIFE.

Jesus' life testifies to the accuracy of the prophet's words. He preached "good news to the poor." His grace—the good news of the gospel—lifts those who are broken, bruised, and crushed with guilt. He offers new beginnings and heals the brokenhearted. Those who have seen their loved ones swallowed by the jaws of death find reassurance in Christ, who was resurrected from the dead. Drying their tears, He gives them hope for tomorrow. In Jesus, death is not the end of the road. A glorious resurrection day awaits us.

Some time ago a person in Sydney, Australia, placed a sign over the door of his shop: "Everything mended here except broken hearts." This skilled individual could fix washing machines, televisions, radios, cars, and bicycles, but not broken people. But what repair shops cannot do Jesus can. No problem is too great for Him to solve, no difficulty too hard for Him to unravel. As Isaiah said of Jesus: "He has sent me . . . to proclaim freedom for the captives and release from darkness for the prisoners" (verse 1).

Down through the centuries Jesus has proved capable of setting every kind of captive free. He is the great liberator, whether someone is shackled to alcohol and drugs; in bondage to lust, greed, selfishness, and anger; or locked in prisons of despair, discouragement, and depression.

Let me give you a dramatic example. A young woman named Eileen entered the hospital convinced that she had multiple sclerosis. In fact, she showed many of the symptoms. But neurological tests revealed no traces of the disease. When psychiatrist William Wilson told her about the test findings, she became angry. Eileen still continued to insist that she did have multiple sclerosis.

During later visits Dr. Wilson discovered that the young woman was really suffering from a long bout with depression. She had a lot of anxiety and stress in her life. But for Eileen, having a physical problem seemed a whole lot better than a mental one.

Dr. Wilson had come to believe that a relationship with God can help in a person's healing. The idea also intrigued Eileen. She wanted to know how she could have a Christ-centered life. So the psychiatrist talked about learning how to trust Jesus as Savior and to surrender one's will to Christ as Lord.

A RELATIONSHIP WITH GOD CAN HELP IN A PERSON'S HEALING FROM THE INJURIES OF LIFE.

Here is Revelation's key to receiving the liberating power of the Spirit that Eileen needed: "Whoever is thirsty, let him come; and whoever wishes, let him take the free gift of the water of life" (Revelation 22:17).

The physician explained to Eileen that as she consciously surrendered to the lordship of Jesus Christ, a wonderful change would take place in her whole life. About a week later she asked Jesus to enter her life. And she prayed to be filled with the Holy Spirit. After that, Dr. Wilson encouraged her to ask God for wisdom to understand her illness—whatever it was. As Eileen prayed, her depression suddenly intensified. But in her pain she finally began to realize that her real problem was the depression, not the multiple sclerosis she was so sure she had.

Dr. Wilson continued counseling and praying with her. Her symptoms began to disappear, and soon she was ready to go home.

But after she was back at the house and surrounded by her old environment, that horrible feeling of depression began to overwhelm her again, leaving her nauseated. For two hours she struggled with it, until finally she collapsed to the floor, unable to move. It seemed that all her old symptoms were back.

But at that moment something struck her—a revelation. She realized that deep inside she hadn't fully surrendered her will to Him. So Eileen cried out, "I give up." She asked God to forgive her pride and to enable her to serve Him. Before long she began to face each day with anticipation and joy.

PROPHECIES FULFILLED IN JESUS' LAST HOURS

The most precise prophecies about the Messiah were fulfilled during the final 24 hours of Jesus' life. They offer evidence for those open-minded enough to honestly consider who He really is.

The prophet Zechariah predicted that the Messiah would ride into Jerusalem on a donkey (Zechariah 9:9). Passion Week began with Jesus' triumphant entry into the city on a donkey, as the prophet foretold. The Gospel writer Mark confirms the fulfillment of the prediction: "They brought the colt to Jesus and threw their cloaks over it" (Mark 11:7).

In addition, the prophets of the Old Testament indicate that:

1. Jesus as Messiah would remain silent in suffering (Isaiah 53:7).
2. Jesus would be whipped, smitten, and flogged (Isaiah 50:5, 6).
3. Jesus would be executed (Zechariah 12:10).

Death has claimed the world's great leaders down through the ages. Abraham Lincoln, George Washington, Vladimir Lenin, Mao Tse-tung, Winston Churchill, Charlemagne, Napoleon, Alexander the Great, and a host of others who have commanded some of the world's largest armies and ruled some of the world's greatest empires are buried, and their bodies have crumbled away. Their voices are silent—their powerful influence largely gone.

But the Christ of prophecy is different. Jesus' tomb is empty—He is alive. And because He is alive, His offer of eternal life is real. His promise of forgiveness is genuine. And His life-changing power is available to you and me today. Because He rose from the grave, Jesus is still in the business of transforming men and women by His grace.

A miracle of God's grace can take place in your life. You do not need to struggle with the same habits again and again. When life presses you down, when you struggle with impulses that seem uncontrollable, when you feel too weak to try to overcome anything—remember the apostle Paul's words: "In all these things we are more than conquerors through him who loved us" (Romans 8:37).

I can think of no better example than the experience of my own father, James Finley. He was just another New York City slum kid, like thousands of others growing up in what people called Hell's Kitchen. He had no home life to speak of, no money, no future. Dad had to learn about life the hard way—on the streets. And for a long time, it seemed, he absorbed all the wrong lessons.

Siegfried Horn Museum/Nathan Greene

His mother was unstable, and his stepfather earned only a very small income as a part-time tugboat captain. The family constantly had to move, constantly had to scrounge for life's necessities. As a boy, Dad, wearing the khaki pants that announced to the world he was on welfare, had to get used to standing in line for free cans of beans and stew. During an 11-year period he attended 15 different schools. It was almost impossible to keep up with his studies.

One Friday night Dad came home and found that the doorknob on the front door wouldn't turn. Then he noticed a white piece of paper taped there with a message: "We moved. New address: 110th Street, Harlem."

No longer did he have just to endure fights—now he had to watch out for gang wars. And the family's poverty became outright desolation.

Dad picked up more and more signs around the house that he wasn't really wanted. So at the age of 17 he decided to take off on his own. At first he hid out in the home of a friend named Skip. Skip let him stay in the attic and slipped him meals.

MY FATHER'S LIFE SHOWED ME GOD'S POWER TO TRANSFORM.

Later Dad went to live with a stepbrother in Jersey City and managed to find odd jobs here and there. But he'd gotten into the habit of petty theft. He convinced himself that he took only things he really needed.

Finally my father tried what seemed to be the ultimate escape—the Navy. He joined it at the age of 17, and the military discipline did give him a measure of stability. But as a sailor he was mainly interested in freedom—staying out late, going from bar to bar—with no badgering parents around. Eventually he became involved in car theft.

Ultimately my father realized that the constant struggle had become too overwhelming. Sensing an emptiness within, he realized the need for divine power to transform his life. Opening his heart to the power of the living Christ, he surrendered to the claims of the Spirit and let God's life-transforming power begin its work.

Dad didn't just get out of Hell's Kitchen—Hell's Kitchen got out of him as he made the ultimate escape. The barhopping sailor who kept "borrowing" cars became a beloved and respected father and community leader.

The important question, of course, is *How* did it happen? How did such a change come about?

One day Dad dropped to his knees and repeated the words of that hymn to God: "'And though all men should forsake Thee, by Thy grace I'll follow Thee.'" My father escaped from Hell's Kitchen because he truly made a commitment. He stopped saying that he'd like to find out if this religion bit was real—someday. Instead Jim Finley dedicated himself heart and soul to God.

JESUS CAN HELP ANYONE, NO MATTER WHAT THE CIRCUMSTANCES OF THEIR LIVES OR THE PROBLEMS THEY ARE STRUGGLING WITH.

SIEGFRIED HORN MUSEUM/NATHAN GREENE

The Lord of Scripture *is* a God of great transformations. He *can* help people escape the worst circumstances or the narrowest lives. But what makes the difference between just getting out of Hell's Kitchen and Hell's Kitchen getting out of us is the commitment that we make. That's how we become overcomers.

The Holy Spirit is with us for the long haul. He's there for us. The big question is Are you there for Him? Are you allowing God's Spirit into your life? Maybe you're still resisting on some level, as Eileen did for so long. Or perhaps you just want to get rid of the symptoms instead of the cause. It could be that you may be running away from a deeper problem that God wants you to deal with.

Isn't it time to surrender to the Lord, who alone can transform you? Isn't it time to give your will into the hands of the One who can fill you with good things?

CHAPTER 3
STOPPING HITLER IN HIS TRACKS

In 1940 and 1941 Hitler's German military might seemed unstoppable. His panzer division tanks and blitzkrieg ("lightning war") attacks would set a new standard in twentieth-century military warfare. His armies quickly overran Eastern Europe, then plowed through France and the lowland countries. Night after night his bombers pounded London.

In March of 1941 the German leader gave a significant speech to his people, stating, "See, my people, we do not need anything from God! We do not ask anything from Him except that He may let us alone. We want to fight our own war, with our own guns, without God. We want to gain our victory without the help of God."

Hitler arrogantly believed he could conquer Europe with the strength of his armies. And during 1941, who would dare say he was wrong? His predictions of a united Europe under the Nazi regime seemed to be coming true. Who could dare to challenge his claim?

Maxwell predicted Hitler would fail.

Harry Anderson

One man did. Arthur S. Maxwell edited the *Signs of the Times* magazine during the 1940s. Through a series of editorials he forecast the downfall of Hitler and the failed unification of Europe based on a series of prophecies in the second chapter of the book of Daniel. Maxwell was so confident that the prophet Daniel had it right that he featured Hitler's defeat even at the pinnacle of his power on the cover of his magazine. Some of Maxwell's colleagues cautioned him not to be so bold. But he believed God's words. He accepted God's words to the prophet Isaiah: "See, the former things have taken place, and new things I declare; before they spring into being I announce them to you" (Isaiah 42:9). God knows the end from the beginning. He sees the future clearer than we can see even this present moment.

Daniel 2 contains an ancient prophecy that predicted who would rule the biblical world, and then how our world would eventually end. It began when Daniel was alive on earth—when a king dreamed of world events that spanned 2,500 years. They have come to pass with such precision that only the hand of God could have shaped them. The prophecy demonstrates that God is in control of history. Daniel's prophecy has been almost totally fulfilled—almost, but not quite. But when you glance back over more than 2,000 years of completed prophecy, you can look ahead with assurance at the last little bit that remains to be fulfilled.

DANIEL 2 PREDICTS WHO WILL RULE THE WORLD AND HOW IT WILL END.

Let's listen as Daniel tells his story: "In the second year of his reign, Nebuchadnezzar had dreams; his mind was troubled and he could not sleep" (Daniel 2:1).

MAGNIFICENT BABYLON

Nebuchadnezzar II ruled the great Neo-Babylonian Empire from the massive walled city (circumference of 19 miles) of Babylon more than 600 years before Christ. The city straddled the Euphrates River. Flowing under the walls and through the city, the river provided a constant water supply. The Greek historian Herodotus reports that the city also maintained large food reserves. The walls of Babylon were so thick that two chariots could race side by side on them. Nebuchadnezzar built the city's luxurious hanging gardens—one of the Seven Wonders of the Ancient

DAVID MERLING

BABYLON, HERE SYBOLIZED BY THIS LION MADE UP OF TILES ON A WALL, WAS THE FIRST KINGDOM IN THE KING'S DREAM OF THE IMAGE.

World—for his Median wife who had grown up in the mountains and now missed her homeland. On these terraced gardens fragrant flowers and fruit trees blossomed, and water cascaded through an extremely advanced irrigation system.

In an inscription found in the ruins of the city Nebuchadnezzar boasts, "I have made Babylon, the holy city, the glory of the great gods, more prominent than before, and have promoted its rebuilding. I have caused the sanctuaries of gods and goddesses to lighten up like the day. No king among all kings has ever created, no earlier king has ever built, what I have magnificently built for Marduk."

At the center of Babylon, according to the ancient historian Herodotus, rose the temple tower of Etemenanki. Three hundred feet square at the base, it stood nearly 300 feet high. One of its shrines contained a golden figure of the god Marduk sitting on a throne. Also the Babylonians used much gold to decorate the city.

A MYSTERIOUS DREAM

One night amid all of his opulence, success, and power, the king had a dream he could not remember. I'm sure you can relate to his experience—waking up in the morning, knowing that you had a dream and trying in vain to remember it. But I doubt if you ever took it to the extreme that Nebuchadnezzar did. The Bible tells us that he called together his magicians, astrologers, and wise men and asked *them* to tell *him* what he had dreamed. "O king, live forever!" they replied. "Tell your servants the dream, and we will interpret it" (Daniel 2:4). They figured they could analyze the dream and make up some sort of interpretation once they knew what it had been about. But interpretation wasn't the problem—remembering it was!

Their response upset Nebuchadnezzar. Recognizing what they were trying to do, he demanded, "Tell me the dream, and I will know that you can interpret it for me" (verse 9). If you can't tell me the dream, the king was saying, how am I supposed to trust you to give me its meaning? You're supposed to be able to see into the future! Prove it to me now. Tell me what I dreamed.

"There is not a man on earth who can do what the king asks," his advisors protested. But Nebuchadnezzar would not back off. Somehow he sensed his dream was important, and he was desperate to know what it meant. The king became so angry that he decreed that if his counselors could not tell him his dream and its interpretation, he would kill them all.

THE DREAM ADVANCED GENERATION AFTER GENERATION UNTIL THE CLOSE OF HISTORY.

Arioch, the king's captain, came to execute Daniel. The Babylonian forces had taken Daniel captive when they attacked Jerusalem. Although he was not one of Babylon's psychics, he was one of the city's educated elite, trained as a servant for the king and thus regarded as a "wise man." Now, when Daniel asked why he must die, Arioch told him the story of the dream. The Bible says that the Israelite captive went in to see the king and asked for time so that he could pray to the God of heaven, who reveals all secrets. He had utmost confidence that the Lord of Israel would solve the problem.

During a night vision God did reveal the dream and its interpretation. Afterward Daniel offered a wonderful prayer of thanks to Him. "I thank and praise you," he said. "You have given me wisdom and power" (verse 23). The prophet did not claim any of the glory for himself. Knowing where any wisdom he had came from, he sincerely thanked the God of heaven.

DANIEL TOLD NEBUCHADNEZZAR, "AFTER YOU, ANOTHER KINGDOM WILL RISE."

And then Daniel told the king that no wise man, no astrologer, no magician, no soothsayer, could reveal the dream. "But there is a God in heaven who reveals mysteries," the prophet declared. "He has shown King Nebuchadnezzar what will happen in days to come" (verse 28). God was very clear with Daniel that the king's dream had actually revealed events that would occur up to the last days of earth's history. The dream starts with Nebuchadnezzar's lifetime, and it advances generation after generation after generation until the close of human history.

The prophet next reminded the king what he had dreamed. "You looked, O king, and there before you stood a large statue—an enormous, dazzling statue, awesome in appearance. The head of the statue was made of pure gold, its chest and arms of silver, its belly and thighs of bronze, its legs of iron, its feet partly of iron and partly of baked clay. While you were watching, a rock was cut out, but not by human hands. It struck the statue on its feet of iron and clay and smashed them. Then the iron, the clay, the bronze, the silver and the gold were broken to pieces at the same time and became like chaff on a threshing floor in the summer. The wind swept them away without leaving a trace. But the rock that struck the statue became a huge mountain and filled the whole earth" (verses 31-35).

"Yes, that's it! That's it!" the king exclaimed. "That's exactly what I saw! But Daniel, what does it mean?"

Did the Hebrew captive begin to stutter and say, "Well, I know what you dreamed, but I don't know what it means"? Of course not! God revealed not only the content of the dream but also the interpretation. It was a dream not only for Nebuchadnezzar but for us as well, and God has made it simple for us to understand. Note how Daniel began the interpretation: "You, O king, are the king of kings. . . . You are that head of gold" (verses 37, 38).

BABYLON

History books tell us that the Babylonian Empire was the dominant world power from 605 B.C. to 539 B.C. They also note that King Nebuchadnezzar's kingdom was splashed with gold. Remember how lavishly he used it in Marduk's temple? That one temple alone contained tons of gold. I can think of no better way for God to describe the Babylonian Empire than through the symbolism of gold.

Nebuchadnezzar declared, "Babylon—the city which is the delight of my eyes, and which I have glorified; may it last forever."

Nebuchadnezzar was happy with the interpretation. He liked being the head of gold. In fact, he wanted the head of gold to last forever. His ambition was to establish a kingdom that would reign for millennia. Archaeologists have unearthed an inscription he had stamped on one of Babylon's clay tablets: "Babylon—the city which is the delight of my eyes, and which I have glorified; may it last forever."

But God had other plans. The prophet Daniel continues explaining the dream: "After you, another kingdom will rise" (verse 39).

MEDO-PERSIA

At the time Nebuchadnezzar had his dream he was secure as a world leader, with no reason to suspect that it would not always be so. But the

JAMES CONVERSE

DANIEL'S INTERPRETATION OF THE WORDS WRITTEN ON THE WALL SPELLED IMPENDING DOOM FOR THE MIGHTY BABYLONIAN EMPIRE.

dream foretold that he would be overthrown by a kingdom represented in Daniel 2:32 as the "chest and arms of silver." Daniel 5:28 refers to the next ancient Near Eastern power as "the Medes and Persians." Again, the dream has a fitting symbol: the two arms to show two kingdoms—Medes and Persians. The Medes and Persians ruled much of the ancient Near East from 539 B.C. to 331 B.C.

Daniel 5 relates the story of the collapse of the Babylonian rule. Belshazzar, coruler with his father, King Nabonidus, and grandson of King Nebuchadnezzar, hosted a feast for a thousand of his lords. He called for servants to bring to him the gold and silver vessels captured from the Temple in Jerusalem. From these vessels once used in Temple services to worship the God of heaven, he now drank wine. In the midst of his drunken party, a mysterious hand appeared and wrote words on the wall: "MENE, MENE, TEKEL, PARSIN."

Their interpretation spelled doom for the mighty Babylonian Empire: "Mene: God has numbered the days of your reign and brought it to an end. Tekel: You have been weighed on the scales and found wanting.

Peres: Your kingdom is divided and given to the Medes and Persians" (verses 26-28).

That very night, tradition says, the Medes and Persians diverted the Euphrates River that ran under the massive walls of Babylon. (Another tradition suggests that the people of the city opened the gates to the Medo-Persian armies.) They marched their armies straight down the empty riverbed and came up inside the city. Some 150 years in advance Isaiah 44:24 through 45:13 not only told how quickly Babylon would fall, but also named the leader who would conquer it—Cyrus. The Medo-Persian army, led by Cyrus, overwhelmed the city on October 12, 539 B.C., just as the Bible predicted.

ALTHOUGH THE MEDO-PERSIAN EMPIRE ONCE DOMINATED THE BIBLICAL WORLD, ONLY RUINS OF ITS PALACES AND CITIES SURVIVE.

If you visit the British Museum in London, England, you will see one of the most amazing archaeological discoveries of all time. The Cyrus Cylinder is a clay cylinder recording the Persian attack on Babylon. It clearly reveals the name of the Persian king who engineered Babylon's overthrow—Cyrus—and describes how easily the city fell to the invaders. The document even mentions that Cyrus allowed people whom the Babylonians had taken captive (which would include those from Judah) to return to their homelands. Thus the historical record confirms the authenticity of Isaiah's prophecy in Isaiah 44:28 and 45:1.

SIEGFRIED HORN MUSEUM

This remarkable prophecy named Cyrus as the Persian ruler who would overthrow Babylon. Furthermore, it foretold how he

SIEGFRIED HORN MUSEUM

THE CYRUS CYLINDER RECORDS HIS POLICY THAT WOULD EVENTUALLY ALLOW GOD'S PEOPLE TO RETURN TO JERUSALEM.

would accomplish the task. The prophecy clearly delineated that Cyrus would "dry up" Babylon's rivers (Isaiah 44:27), perhaps by diverting them into irrigation canals. It goes on to predict that the Persian king would pass a decree that would allow the Israelites in captivity to return to Jerusalem to rebuild the Temple (verse 28). Events precisely fulfilled the details of the prophecy.

The clay Cyrus Cylinder thus not only chronicles the Persian king's attack on Babylon, but confirms the authenticity of prophecy. It reveals for all generations that:

Cyrus did overthrow Babylon.

Cyrus took the city without a battle.

Cyrus did establish a policy that would eventually allow God's people to return to Jerusalem.

The Medes and Persians ruled the world for nearly two centuries. But Nebuchadnezzar's dream didn't end there, and neither did history. Time marches on, one kingdom replacing another, just as God had foretold.

GREECE

The next kingdom Daniel 2:32 portrays through the symbolism of the belly and thighs of bronze. More than 200 years in advance Daniel actually named Greece as this third kingdom, which overthrew the Medes and the Persians (Daniel 8:21). Once again we find an appropriate representation. Alexander the Great, a young man, marched his men 11,000 miles, conquering almost all of the then-known world before he died, probably of malaria, about a month before he turned 33. What did his soldiers take into battle? Bronze breastplates, bronze helmets, bronze shields, and bronze battle-axes. Once again, God chose a fitting metaphor to describe the kingdom that would rule the world from 331 B.C. to 168 B.C.

Siegfried Horn Museum

The Parthenon has become the symbol of Greek civilization that Alexander the Great spread across the ancient world.

But history doesn't end with the third kingdom. Greece did not last forever, for the image in the dream contained a fourth metal after the gold of Babylon, the silver of the Medes and Persians, and the bronze of Greece. Iron symbolizes the next kingdom. "Finally, there will be a fourth kingdom, strong as iron" (Daniel 2:40).

ROME

The last kingdom to rule the ancient Mediterranean world the vision portrays as iron. In 168 B.C. Rome overthrew the Greeks. So inescapably did the prophetic portrayal correspond to its historical fulfillment that the English historian Edward Gibbon, though not a Christian or Bible believer himself, used scriptural language in his monumental *History of the Decline and Fall of the Roman Empire* when he wrote: "The images of gold, or silver, or brass, that might serve to represent the nations and their kings, were successively broken by the *iron* monarchy of Rome."

Just as legs form the longest part of the body, so Rome had the longest reign of any of the ancient powers depicted by the dream. Little by little

Siegfried Horn Museum

The Colosseum, a symbol of Roman imperial power

the kingdom of Rome expanded and gained strength, fighting many wars and conquering many people. By the time of Jesus' birth most of the Mediterranean world was under Roman rule. You will remember that Joseph and Mary were on their way to pay taxes to the Roman ruler Caesar Augustus when Jesus was born.

For more than 500 years Rome appeared to be invincible—its banners waving from the Atlantic Ocean to the Euphrates River and beyond. But were the Romans the last ruling empire of the world known by the people of the Bible? What did the Bible predict?

Daniel wrote: "Just as you saw that the feet and toes were partly of baked clay and partly of iron, so this will be a divided kingdom" (Daniel 2:41).

A DIVIDED EMPIRE

How did the Roman Empire break up? Did it collapse before the onslaught of an even stronger kingdom, as had happened during the preceding 1,000 years? If this prophecy is to be right, it must predict what actually happened in history—that the legs of iron would *not* be succeeded by a fifth power that controlled the same region.

History confirms that the seemingly unconquerable Roman Empire crumbled two ways—from within and from without. Wealth poured into Rome through taxes and booty collected from throughout the empire. Luxury and pomp replaced the simple Roman life. The political world brewed with corruption, crime infiltrated the streets, and sexual immorality became rampant. And as the mighty Roman Empire weakened from within, Rome faced attack from without and eventually fragmented into what would become some of the modern nations of Western and Eastern Europe.

Daniel 2:42 predicted history from the time of the downfall of the Roman Empire to the end of time. Describing the divisions of the Roman Empire, the prophet declares, "This kingdom will be partly strong and partly brittle." Throughout the centuries some of the nations of the lands bordering the Mediterranean Sea have been extremely powerful, while others have been weak militarily, economically, and politically. The prophecy continues with these insightful words: "They will mingle with the seed of men; but they will not adhere to one another" (verse 43, NKJV). What does the prophet mean? Political leaders in this region of the world have attempted to unite in essentially three ways:

> PROPHECY SAYS, "THEY WILL NOT ADHERE TO ONE ANOTHER."

1. Politically through war.
2. Economically through common currencies, trade agreements, and revenue sharing.
3. Socially through the intermarriage of their offspring. For example, Napoleon divorced Josephine and married Maria Louisa of Austria to unite the Napoleonic line with the Hapsburg dynasty in an attempt to bring Europe together. He declared, "There will be a European System, a European Code of Law, a European Court of

> Appeals. . . . There will be one Europe." But God's Word said that "they will not adhere." The lands of the old Roman Empire would never be permanently reunited again, no matter what Napoleon, Hitler, or anyone else desired.

No matter how many battles humanity fights, no matter how many Hitlers try to conquer the Mediterranean world, they will not succeed. The Bible says that just as iron and clay will not mix together, so Eastern and Western Europe will not be united under one ruler again.

Why is it important that you know about the dream of an ancient king? Simply this—the image in Nebuchadnezzar's dream portrayed the time line of history down to our day. Once you realize that you can have confidence in the Bible about the past, you will know without a doubt that you can also trust Scripture about things still to come.

Where are we living today? In the toenails of history! Every part of this prophecy has come to pass except for one: "While you were watching, a rock was cut out, but not by human hands. It struck the statue on its feet of iron and clay and smashed them. . . . The God of heaven will set up a kingdom that will never be destroyed. . . . It will crush all those kingdoms and bring them to an end, but it will itself endure forever" (verses 34-44).

GOD IN CONTROL

History has followed this prophecy like a blueprint and will continue to do so. The political workings of our planet are not random. God has been guiding and controlling it all along, and only one kingdom remains to rule the world—His kingdom. That rock, cut out without hands, is the one kingdom that will endure forever.

John, in the book of Revelation, speaks about this coming world: "And there were loud voices in heaven, which said: 'The kingdom of the world has become the kingdom of our Lord and of his Christ, and he will reign for ever and ever'" (Revelation 11:15). The final superpower will be divine.

Today we can have hope, because tomorrow is in the hands of the

THE GOD OF DANIEL IN EACH CHAPTER OF THE BOOK	
CHAPTER 1	The God who turns defeat into victory.
CHAPTER 2	The God who reveals the future.
CHAPTER 3	The God who redeems His people.
CHAPTER 4	The God who rules over all.
CHAPTER 5	The God of justice and judgment.
CHAPTER 6	The God who is steadfast forever.
CHAPTER 7	The God whose kingdom triumphs.
CHAPTER 8	The God whose truth triumphs.
CHAPTER 9	The God who keeps His covenant.
CHAPTER 10	The God who hears every prayer.
CHAPTER 11	The God whose people triumph.
CHAPTER 12	The God whose purposes triumph.

same God who has been guiding history from one end of the time line to the other.

Arthur S. Maxwell, and thousands like him, believed God's Word with simple faith. They trusted a God who was in control of the future no matter what the political landscape looked like.

History has played itself out. Only one kingdom remains to be established. Soon Jesus Christ, the one who came to our planet 2,000 years ago, will pay us yet another visit. And He is going to make a grand entrance the second time.

CHAPTER 4

LONGING FOR A HOME

Rwanda is a small, landlocked, mountainous country in east-central Africa. Most people remember the nation for its horrific genocide that killed more than 800,000 people in 1994. Recently I visited Rwanda to share the message of God's love and the Bible's hopeful prophecies about the future.

One evening after my presentation in the capital city of Kigali, a young boy stopped me as I was leaving the auditorium. He must have been 8, maybe 9 years old. With a touch of sadness in his voice he said, "Sir, I have no daddy. Would you be my daddy?" Orphans throng Kigali's city streets. They often beg for a few cents to survive.

But this lad moved me to the core of my being. Putting my arm around his shoulder, I gently said, "Son, you have a heavenly Father much, much better than I. One day He will send His Son, Jesus, to take you home. You will never be lonely or experience hunger again. No longer will you have to roam these streets begging. He loves you and is coming again for you." We hugged. The boy smiled as if to say, I understand. A faint glimmer of hope pierced the darkness of his life. The thought of our Lord's return lifted his spirits.

The second coming of Christ is more than some boring religious dogma. To millions it is the one thing that keeps them going day after day. The return of our Lord has buoyed the spirits of people of all ages for centuries. It gives hope for:

- the young couple whose first child was born dead.

- the wife whose husband died from lung cancer.
- the parents whose daughter was killed by a drunk driver.
- the parents whose son was gunned down in a gangland slaying.
- the survivors of earthquakes, floods, and tornadoes who long to be reunited with the loved ones who perished in the natural disaster.

Bible prophecy foretells the return of our Lord 1,500 times. A reference to it appears, on average, once in every 25 verses of the New Testament. For every prophecy about the first coming of Christ in the Old Testament, we find eight referring to His second coming.

THE SECOND COMING IS A CERTAINTY

For the Bible writers, the return of our Lord was a certainty. The apostle Paul declares, "The Lord himself will come down from heaven" (1 Thessalonians 4:16). The angels testify, "This same Jesus . . . will come back in the same way you have seen him go into heaven" (Acts 1:11). Jesus Himself promised, "I will come back" (John 14:3).

The second advent of Christ is one of the most prominent themes of the New Testament. It's the blessed hope of every Christian. Yet many Bible-believing churchgoers are totally misled on this subject. Unwittingly they have accepted a counterfeit concept that has no biblical foundation. They have read books about prophecy rather than the teachings of the Bible itself. Satan is preparing their minds for his greatest deception ever.

SATAN, THE IMPERSONATOR

One way Satan wants to detour every hoping Christian is to set us up for a bold, convincing impersonation of the Second Coming. Could this really be possible? The Bible says it *will* be!

Satan—the devil—is a fallen angel with awesome supernatural powers. God's Word does its best to warn us in 2 Corinthians 11:14 that "Satan himself masquerades as an angel of light." Once heaven's highest angel, Lucifer, the devil won't hesitate to pass himself off as the brilliant, magnetic angel he once was.

FALSE MIRACLES

The Bible says in the last days Satan will deceive humanity through his power.

"They are spirits of demons performing miraculous signs, and they go out to the kings of the whole world."

—REVELATION 16:14

That's why Jesus, after talking to His disciples about His second coming, warned in Matthew 24:25, 26: "See, I have told you ahead of time. So if anyone tells you, 'There he is, out in the desert,' do not go out; or, 'Here he is, in the inner rooms,' do not believe it." Jesus knew that Satan would attempt to impersonate Him.

And Revelation 12:12 warns, "Woe to the earth . . . because the devil has gone down to you! He is filled with fury, because he knows that his time is short." The shorter the time to Jesus' return, the greater Satan's motivation to deceive the human race will become. As time runs out, he will become more desperate to fool millions with a false second coming.

Imagine that a cry went out, "Christ is in San Francisco or Moscow or São Paulo or Nairobi or Rome. He's walking the streets, reaching out His hands to everyone. Thousands are coming to Him, and He's healing them of cancer and countless other illnesses. Come to Christ!"

Would you go? How would you know if this were the true Christ or the devil himself? Someone says, "Oh, Satan could never work miracles. That's how I'd know." And someone else might assume, "Satan could never heal people of cancer or blindness—only God can do that."

Don't be so sure. The book of Revelation warns the last generation of Christians about "spirits of demons performing miraculous signs, and they go out to the kings of the whole world" (Revelation 16:14).

The devil can perform miracles—that's what the Bible says. If he, for example, made people sick in the first place, he could then simply withdraw his hand and apparently heal them.

Now, don't misunderstand me. God does work miracles Himself. Because of that fact, Satan will through his own supernatural powers seek to counterfeit them as a way of deceiving people. And when Satan, at the end of time, appears on earth as a being of dazzling brightness and claims he's going to set up his kingdom on earth, will he repeat some of Jesus' beautiful words and work miracles to trick humanity? Indeed he will! That's what the Bible warns us against.

The apostle Paul sounds an urgent alarm about the one "whose coming is after the working of Satan with all power and signs and lying wonders" (2 Thessalonians 2:9, KJV). Satan masqueraded in the Garden of Eden as a kind benefactor of the human race. He deluded Eve into thinking he had her best good in mind. Again Satan will attempt to persuade millions into believing that he is the originator of all good things. He will do that through miraculous signs and awesome wonders.

How can you and I avoid his last-day delusions? Only by knowing what the Bible really teaches about Christ's second coming. God will never allow Satan to counterfeit the genuine return of Jesus—that is beyond even his diabolical power. So if we understand how Christ is going to come—and Bible writers clearly tell us just how He will return—we won't be deceived.

SATAN THE COUNTERFEITER

But before I share with you what biblical prophets have told us about the genuine return of Jesus, I want to warn you about the second way Satan will try to counteract the Second Coming. Besides impersonation, he will also come up with erroneous theories about how it will happen. In fact, he already has—and millions have been swept up by them. In the Western world the most popular one is the doctrine of the secret rapture. Entire denominations teach it as truth. The best-selling Left Behind book series builds upon it. We hear it preached all over religious television. But it's simply not in the Bible!

According to the teachings about the rapture, seven years before the second coming of Christ, Jesus secretly returns to earth and snatches away His followers, taking them back to heaven with Him. Those who still remain will go through seven years of tribulation. But it will give them a second chance at salvation.

Halfway through the seven years an evil, powerful man called the antichrist will become the ruler of the world. He will have all of his followers identified in a special way (the mark of the beast), perhaps a computer chip embedded in a person's forehead or hand. At the end of the seven years Jesus comes back once more and sets up His kingdom here on earth, where He rules for 1,000 years.

Amazingly, millions today believe in the secret rapture, even though rapturists base it on only two or three misconstrued verses.

THE BIBLE HAS NOTHING IN IT ABOUT AN INVISIBLE OR SECRET COMING OF CHRIST.

What the Bible does say about God is that he does *nothing* secretly. "Surely the Sovereign Lord does nothing without revealing his plan to his servants the prophets" (Amos 3:7). If God is about to do something, He doesn't keep it hidden. He tells His prophets what will happen—and they in turn communicate it to God's people. And He especially wouldn't keep secret the greatest future event yet to take place in human history. The Bible has nothing in it about an invisible coming of Christ.

DOES THE BIBLE SUPPORT THE SECRET RAPTURE IDEA?

Let's look at the few texts that supposedly support the secret rapture. The first is in Matthew 24. Here Jesus tells His disciples about His second coming, and in verses 37-41 He declares: "As it was in the days of Noah, so it will be at the coming of the Son of Man. For in the days before the flood, people were eating and drinking, marrying and giving in marriage, up to the day Noah entered the ark; and they knew nothing about what would happen until the flood came and took them all away. That is how it will be at the coming of the Son of Man. Two men will be in the field; one will be taken and the other left. Two women will be grinding with a hand mill; one will be taken and the other left."

Rapturists claim that the passage demonstrates Jesus' secret coming, that He takes one here and one there, and then leaves the others behind.

But notice that the verses do not say that they are left behind *alive*. In fact, the Bible says in 2 Thessalonians 2:8 that at the Second Coming the forces of evil and wickedness—which would include all who reject Christ—He shall "destroy by the splendor of his coming."

Luke 17 gives us a detailed description of the two classes alive at the return of our Lord. Noah's day had two classes: the saved and the lost. Lot in Sodom encountered those same two classes. And in both times those "left behind" were not alive. They perished (Luke 17:27, 29). Jesus makes it too plain to be misunderstood when He says, "It will be just like this on the day the Son of Man is revealed" (verse 30).

The issue in Luke 17 is whether you save your life or lose it (verse 33). Right after the passage "two men will be in the field; one will be taken and the other left" (verse 36), some of Jesus' listeners raised the question "Where, Lord?" (verse 37). In other words, what happens to the class left behind? The answer is plain: "Where there is a dead body, there the vultures will gather" (verse 37). Revelation 19:21 tells us that those left behind are slain and birds eat their flesh. No one has a second chance after Jesus comes.

A second passage used to support a secret rapture is 1 Corinthians 15:51-53. "Listen, I tell you a mystery," Paul wrote. "We will not all sleep, but we will all be changed—in a flash, in the twinkling of an eye, at the last trumpet. For the trumpet will sound, the dead will be raised imperishable, and we will be changed. For the perishable must clothe itself with the imperishable, and the mortal with immortality."

Rapturists focus on the words "changed—in a flash, in the twinkling of an eye" and see that as the moment of the rapture. But notice that this passage about the Second Coming declares that it will happen "at the last trumpet" and that "the trumpet will sound." How could even Jesus keep His return secret with a trumpet blaring to announce it?

> THE PEOPLE BEFORE THE FLOOD IGNORED NOAH'S WARNING UNTIL IT WAS TOO LATE.

Finally, rapturists claim support from one final text. First Thessalonians 4:16-18: "For the Lord himself will come down from heaven, with a loud command, with the voice of the archangel and with the trumpet call of God, and the dead in Christ will rise first. After that, we who are still alive and are left will be caught up together with them in the clouds to meet the Lord in the air. And so we will be with the Lord forever. Therefore encourage each other with these words."

Again rapturists concentrate on just a few words of the passage, ignoring their context. They highlight "we who are still alive and are left will be caught up." Actually, it is from this text in its ancient Latin translation that the word "rapture" (from the Latin word *raptus*, for "caught up" or "carried away") originally derived. But rapture is simply that—a catching upward or a carrying away. Does rapture have implications of secrecy? Not at all.

Notice the context. All those who have died in Christ through all of history God now resurrects from their graves and resting places. Paul refers to the voice of the archangel and the trumpet of God, both ways of publicly announcing that something important is happening. A secret coming? Hardly! God wants everyone to know that it is going on. If Jesus wanted to sneak down to earth and secretly snatch away His followers, He certainly wouldn't sabotage His own intentions with trumpet blasts and loud angel voices!

The roots of the rapture teaching reach all the way back to the Reformation, when the established church launched what historians came to call a Counter-Reformation to contend with Martin Luther and other Reformers.

Later religious leaders arose who experienced "visions" that moved the teaching forward, and little by little other elements merged into it to create an entire system of doctrine that simply doesn't appear in the Bible.

WHAT DIFFERENCE DOES IT MAKE?

You may be wondering What difference does it really make whether we believe in the rapture or not? The answer is simply this: If we are convinced that those of us who love Jesus and look forward to His return at the Second Coming still have a second chance to be saved if we miss the rapture, we may delay our decision for Christ. We may not feel as much

João Luiz Cardozo

urgency to be ready to meet Him. It's like that old saying: "Don't worry if you miss the bus—there's always another one coming along." (Some rapturists do believe, however, that those who reject Christ before the rapture will have already decided their eternal fate.)

But the Bible says that there is no other bus. If we are not ready for Jesus when He does return—if we have not chosen Him daily as our Lord and Savior—we will be lost forever. There *is* no second chance. Can you see what a masterful counterfeit such a doctrine really is? It's a teaching that plays with the eternal destinies of men and women. And do you really want to take chances with your own personal destiny?

Well, then, if the Bible doesn't teach the rapture, what *does* it reveal about the second coming of Jesus? What will that event be like? Let's look at just a few of the Bible references to the Second Coming. Titus 2:13 declares that Christ's return will be glorious. We who love Jesus, Paul wrote, are waiting "for the blessed hope—the glorious appearing of our great God and Savior, Jesus Christ."

HOW THE SECOND COMING OF JESUS WILL BE

The theme of the glorious return of our Lord runs all through Scripture. Jesus puts it this way: "For the Son of Man is going to come in his Father's glory with his angels, and then he will reward each person according to what he has done" (Matthew 16:27). At the Second Coming the entire world will witness the majesty of His appearing. He arrives as "King of kings and Lord of lords" (Revelation 19:16).

The entire world will witness the second coming of Jesus when He arrives to reign as King of kings.

The Bible also teaches that the second coming of Christ is a visible event. Both the saved and lost will witness it. Revelation 1:7 announces: "He is coming with the clouds, and every eye will see him." And our Lord declares in Matthew 24:30: "And all the nations of the earth will mourn. They will see the Son of Man coming on the clouds of the sky, with power and

ASSUMPTIONS OF THE SECRET RAPTURE

1 **Proponents of the secret rapture assume that the rapture is an invisible event seen only by the saved.**

- The Bible teaches that the return of our Lord is a visible event (Revelation 1:7) witnessed by both the saved and unsaved (Matthew 16:24-28; Matthew 24:30, 31; 1 Thessalonians 4:16, 17).

2 **Proponents of the secret rapture assume that the return of our Lord divides into two comings seven years apart.**

- The Bible teaches the return of our Lord is the decisive moment of human history for both the righteous and the wicked (Matthew 13:30, 39-43; Revelation 22:11, 12).

3 **Proponents of the secret rapture believe that those left behind are alive.**

- The Bible teaches that the brightness of our Lord's glorious return destroys those left behind (2 Thessalonians 1:7-9; 2 Thessalonians 2:8; Luke 17:24-37; Matthew 24:45-51; Revelation 6:14-17).

4 **The proponents of the secret rapture assume that the unsaved who go through the tribulation will have a second chance at salvation.**

- The Bible teaches that the only opportunity for salvation is to choose Jesus now (Revelation 22:11; Hebrews 3:7; 2 Corinthians 6:2; Hebrews 9:27, 28).

great glory." Our Lord arrived silently once—unnoticed by the world's leaders, unrecognized by the masses of people, born as an infant in a stable. This time He will arrive as a triumphant king seen by all.

Yes, the return of Jesus will be visible to everyone. Jesus tells us in Matthew 24:27: "For as lightning that comes from the east is visible even in the west, so will be the coming of the Son of Man." Is there anything secret or invisible or silent about lightning? We hear that booming thunder roll majestically in the heavens. The flash of lightning brightens the night sky all across the horizon.

THEORY COMPARED WITH THE BIBLE

Proponents of the secret rapture believe that the people of God—the saved—do not go through the final tribulation. • The Bible teaches that God protects His people through earth's final crisis as they learn to trust Him with a deepening faith (Psalm 91; Psalm 46; Revelation 16:15; Revelation 2:10; Matthew 24:13). • Please note: a. God delivered Israel after the plagues fell upon Egypt. Israel went though the plagues protected by God. b. God delivered the Hebrew captives in Babylon after they met the test of the fiery furnace. They went through the fire protected by God. c. God delivers His people after the seven last plagues. The redeemed too go through protected by God (Revelation 15:8; Revelation 16).	5
Proponents of the secret rapture believe that the rapture occurs before the antichrist reveals himself. • The Bible teaches that first the antichrist is revealed, the mark of the beast is enforced, the tribulation occurs, and only then does our Lord return (2 Thessalonians 2:1-4; Revelation 14:9, 10, 12; Revelation 15:1, 8; Revelation 16:1, 15).	6

Notice something else in 1 Thessalonians 4:17: "After that, we who are still alive and are left will be caught up together with them in the clouds to meet the Lord in the air. And so we will be with the Lord forever." Where do we meet the Lord? "In the air." Does He come all the way down to the earth at this time? Does He walk on our planet as a being of dazzling brightness? Only a false christ—Satan—will do that. The Bible tells us in advance so that we won't be fooled. We'll meet the Lord in the air—we'll be caught up to be with Jesus.

Jesus plainly stated, "And if I go and prepare a place for you, I will come back and take you to be with me that you also may be where I am" (John 14:3). Unlike the rapture doctrine that has Jesus setting up a kingdom as soon as He returns for those left behind on earth and who convert during the seven years of tribulation, He takes us to heaven.

Because some have misinterpreted a few Scripture texts and built up the picture of a secret rapture, in which Christ whisks certain individuals away while others go about their usual business, we need to understand clearly how Jesus described His return:

"But of that day and hour knoweth no man, no, not the angels of heaven, but my Father only" (Matthew 24:36, KJV).

"But understand this: If the owner of the house had known at what time of night the thief was coming, he would have kept watch and would not have let his house be broken into. So you also must be ready, because the Son of Man will come at an hour when you do not expect him" (verses 43, 44).

The secret rapture theory relies primarily on the texts that speak of the Lord coming like a thief in the night. These passages of Scripture emphasize that we must always be ready for the unexpected. On the surface they might seem to imply a secret, perhaps invisible, event. But the problem with such a theory is that these texts stand side by side with passages about Jesus returning in a blaze of glory. Peter mentions the two aspects in the same breath: "But the day of the Lord will come like a thief. The heavens will disappear with a roar; the elements will be destroyed by fire" (2 Peter 3:10).

THE SECOND COMING IS A SURPRISE

Obviously the Lord comes like a thief in the sense that the Second Advent will be a great surprise to those who aren't ready. He catches them off guard. In the ancient world thieves were often lurking outside one's house at night. Only those who refused to remain alert would be surprised when a robber broke into the home. A robbery is not a mystical or invisible event, and neither is the Second Coming. There's nothing quiet or intangible about the heavens disappearing with a roar. It may come as an incredible surprise to those who have ignored God, but the event won't be quiet or secret or mystical.

The Second Coming is the definite, irreversible period that God places at the conclusion of humanity's sinful history on earth. It's the end of one kind of age and the beginning of an entirely new one.

But just as we can't change things after a thief has broken into our home, so sinners will not be able to alter things after Christ bursts through the clouds. Humanity will have no second chance. Getting ready for the Second Coming is not something that we can put off until the right time. When Christ descends from the sky, our destinies will be sealed, our eternal future determined.

So it's vitally important that each of us should follow God's plan, not just our hunches or imaginations. We have to look carefully at what God is going to do.

HITLER LAUNCHED A PREMATURE ATTACK ON POLAND, BUT THE NATION PAID NO ATTENTION TO IT.

World War II officially began on September 1, 1939. But the first shots were actually fired days earlier.

Originally Hitler had planned to launch an attack on Poland on August 26. The evening before, several

PHOTODISC

combat units poised to strike. However, last-minute political developments forced Hitler to postpone the invasion. The German military command had to contact each of the combat units and tell them to wait. But headquarters could not reach one unit.

So at 12:01 a.m. on the appointed day, August 26, a unit led by Lieutenant Herzner moved out and captured a railway station in the town of Mosty. He also took a few Polish prisoners. When Herzner telephoned in his report, he learned that he'd jumped the gun. On orders, he released his prisoners and returned to Germany.

Now, such a premature attack should have made Hitler's intentions plain. But incredibly enough, the Polish government missed the signs, letting the incident pass without notice. And when the Nazis swept the country on September 1, the invasion took the Polish nation by surprise.

SIGNS OF JESUS' RETURN

We don't want to miss the signs of God's final invasion of human history. Scripture describes a cluster of specific events that tells us when Christ's second coming has truly begun. All of them must take place together.

1. Seismic upheavals (Revelation 6:14; 16:18-20).

A great earthquake will shake the planet, moving mountains and islands in the sea.

2. The righteous dead are raised (1 Thessalonians 4:16; John 5:28, 29).

Paul tells us in Thessalonians, "The dead in Christ will rise first." All who sleep in their graves will hear Christ's trumpetlike voice and spring up to immortality.

3. The righteous living are translated (1 Thessalonians 4:17).

The righteous who are still alive will be caught up together with those resurrected from the dead, and both will ascend toward Christ as He flashes across the heavens in glory.

4. Immortality is bestowed (1 Corinthians 15:53).

Both the righteous resurrected dead and the translated living will receive the gift of immortality.

5. The wicked are destroyed (Revelation 19:11-21).

Those who have deliberately and persistently rejected God's call of mercy will perish. The glory of Christ, which is a thrilling sight for His friends, seems like consuming fire to His enemies.

6. The righteous welcome the returning Christ (Isaiah 25:9).

As Christ's followers ascend toward their Lord, their boundless happiness echoes the words of the prophet: "This is our God; we trusted in him, and he saved us. . . . Let us . . . be glad in his salvation."

7. The righteous journey to heaven (John 14:2, 3).

Finally, the righteous begin a wonderful journey with Christ toward their heavenly home. They remember His words of promise: "I am going . . . to prepare a place for you. . . . I will come back and take you to be with me that you also may be where I am."

This is the hope each one of us can cling to if our faith in Christ is secure. It's not something vague or speculative. God has told us exactly how He will return and exactly what will happen when He does.

CHAPTER 5

"THIS JUST IN . . ."

You're watching TV—or maybe just listening as you do other things—when suddenly the broadcast gets interrupted. The words "Breaking News" flash on the screen, and an announcer says, "This just in . . ."

It happens when there's truly urgent or important news:

- a natural disaster.
- the verdict in a major legal trial.
- the results of an important election.
- the death of someone known worldwide.
- an accident or shocking act of terrorism.

Such announcements may involve anything from the loss of a space shuttle . . . to the results of a razor-thin presidential election . . . to the appalling images of September 11, 2001, . . . or the horrible tsunami disaster in Southeast Asia.

When Ted Turner launched CNN in 1980, he said: "We will stay on the air till the end of the world and then we will cover the story and sign off, playing 'Nearer My God to Thee.'"

What bigger news story could anyone possibly imagine than the end of the world? But just *how* will the world end? And even more important—*when?* Could it be that CNN, MSNBC, FOX, ABC, CBS, and NBC should be wasting no time in getting ready for their final broadcast?

At a Harvard faculty dinner early in the previous century, the poet Robert Frost approached Harlow Shapley, one of the founders of modern astronomy, with a blunt and simple question: "How is the world going to end?"

PHOTODISC

Shapley answered as almost any astronomer of that time would have. In about 5 billion years, he explained, the earth will either be incinerated when our sun swells up to be a red giant star—or our world will swing far away from the sun and fall into a deep, permanent ice age.

A few years later, in 1923, Frost penned one of his most famous poems, entitled "Fire and Ice." In it he speculated that the world would end in fire, but should it end two times the second destruction might be by ice.

Two years later another famous American poet named T. S. Eliot also composed a poem that spoke of the world's final end. Entitled "The Hollow Men," the poem concluded that rather than ending with a bang, it would disappear with a whimper.

HOW WILL THE WORLD END?

So how will the world end? Will it perish as the sun expands to consume it? Will it freeze as the earth drifts away from the sun? What about Eliot's suggestion—perishing in the bang of nuclear holocaust or with the whimper of the last starving survivor of a world totally out of resources? Or will the vision of neither poet prevail? Maybe the impact of an asteroid or some worldwide plague or ozone depletion or global warming or some other catastrophe brought on by human pollution of the environment will annihilate all life.

Many do not believe that God made our earth and sun. If they cannot accept how the Lord says the world began, how can they believe what He predicts about its end?

The answer is that they can't. So they find themselves forced to speculate on what cosmic, nuclear, or ecological disaster will finally finish off our world. But God Himself has not remained silent on earth's final destiny. In His Word to us, the Bible, He clearly reveals that the world will not end in fire or ice, a bang or a whimper, even an asteroid collision. It will conclude, He declares, with the return of His Son, Jesus Christ, to this earth in unimaginable glory and power and kingly majesty. As we have already learned, the Bible contains numerous references to the final news story of human history—the second advent of Jesus. If you really

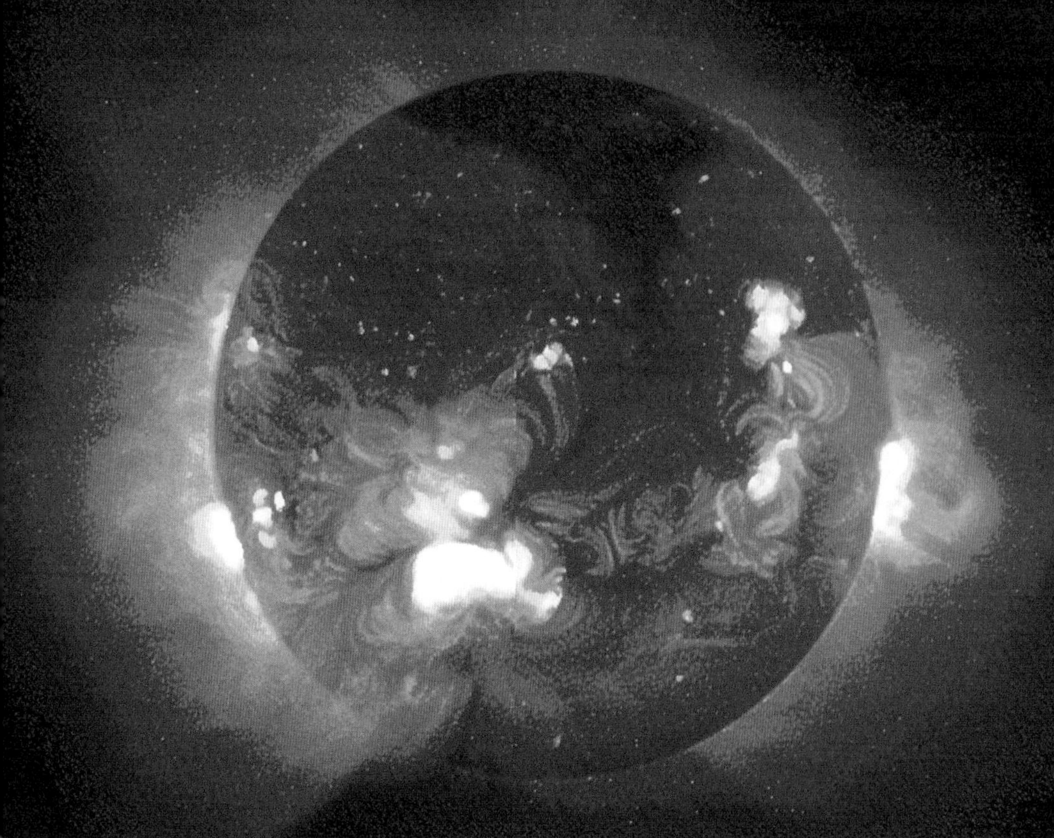

PHOTODISC

want to know about the future, look at what God says. Our Lord's predictions are taking place all around us. The events He foretold some 2,000 years ago are coming to pass with uncanny accuracy.

SOME SCIENTISTS SAY THE SUN WILL SWELL INTO A RED GIANT STAR AND BURN UP THE EARTH.

It is certainly true that no one knows the day or hour of Christ's return (Matthew 24:36). God has not revealed the exact date. Jesus said that even He didn't know. Anyone who claims that Christ is coming at a specific time is mistaken. The supposed dates of Christ's return litter the road of history. But although our Lord has not given the time, He has outlined what will happen beforehand.

One day, the Bible says, as Jesus left the magnificent Temple in the city of Jerusalem, He paused to gaze back at this gold-decorated monument to the highest of Jewish aspirations. Then He said what seemed to be unbelievable. "As for what you see here, the time will come when not one stone will be left on another; every one of them will be thrown down" (Luke 21:6).

A MINIATURE REPLICA OF THE JERUSALEM TEMPLE THAT SO IMPRESSED THE DISCIPLES OF JESUS.

Later, as He sat upon the Mount of Olives, the disciples came to Him privately. "'Tell us,' they said, 'when will this happen?'" (Matthew 24:3). When will Jerusalem be destroyed, they wanted to know—when will the Temple be overthrown? Thinking that the destruction of their awesome Temple could occur only at the end of the world, they also asked a related question: "What will be the sign of Your coming and of the end of the age?" (verse 3).

In a magnificent answer to the disciples' questions, Jesus blended both events—the destruction of the city of Jerusalem by the Roman general Titus in A.D. 70 and the signs leading to the end of the world itself. Many of the events that preceded the destruction of Jerusalem in the first century would repeat themselves on a global scale before the end of the world.

FALSE CHRISTS AND PROPHETS

In Matthew 24 Jesus gave His disciples the signs that would precede His return at the end of human history. They begin in verse 5: "For many will come in my name, claiming, 'I am the Christ,' and will deceive many."

The last days will be characterized by voices coming from different corners of the religious world declaring, "This is the way." "Follow me." "I am a voice from heaven." Many people will claim divine light, prophetic powers, and even equality with the Son of God. Men and women will perform astounding feats and great wonders "to deceive even the elect—if that were possible" (verse 24). Such deceptions will be so

THEODORE CHAMBERLAIN

overwhelming that even God's people, unless they have fortified their minds with the Scriptures, will be misled.

Cult groups have grown explosively throughout the world during recent decades. In survey results first released by *USA Today* in the mid-1990s some 20,000 in a sample group of 113,000 claimed that they accepted the theories of the New Age movement. False religions have increased phenomenally in our generation. Books on the paranormal sell in the multimillions throughout America. Universities offer students classes in nontraditional religions. Many young people who were raised in Christianity have begun to explore non-Christian religions and teachings. Cults especially target those who are searching.

NONE WILL COME PROCLAIMING, "WE ARE FALSE CHRISTS AND FALSE PROPHETS."

Whether it be the New Age movement admonishing its followers to develop the god within them or cult leaders claiming they are divine, the end result is the same deception. The crescendo of interest in alternative religions and the proliferation of religious leaders claiming divine powers reflect the accuracy of our Lord's prediction.

Deception is part of Satan's plan: "They are spirits of demons performing miraculous signs, and they go out to the kings of the whole world, to gather them for the battle on the great day of God Almighty" (Revelation 16:14).

One thing is for certain—such individuals will not come with a sign around their necks saying, "We are false christs and false prophets." They will simply lead, and those who are looking for a leader will follow them.

In March 1997, 39 members of the Heaven's Gate cult produced a farewell video and then took their own lives. They believed that trailing the Hale-Bopp comet was a spacecraft coming to take them to the next level of existence. Investigators found the victims with purple cloths over their heads and shoulders.

In trying to identify the bodies, police set up a toll-free number for relatives to call. In 24 hours they fielded calls from more than 1,500 anguished relatives who had been out of contact with their loved ones for months or even years and suspected they might be part of the cult.

Such false christs and false prophets do not limit themselves to any one part of the world. On the continent of Africa religious leaders who claim to heal the sick and raise the dead have arisen. They present themselves as the new Messiah. Mary David Christ purported to be the reincarnation of divinity in Russia. She attracted more than 15,000 followers whom she called the "White Brotherhood." Central and South America have their share of counterfeit messiahs. Jesus' words are being fulfilled.

WARS AND RUMORS OF WARS

The last days, Jesus went on to explain, would also be characterized by political conflicts. "You will hear of wars and rumors of wars, but see to it that you are not alarmed. Such things must happen, but the end is still to come. Nation will rise against nation, and kingdom against kingdom. There will be famines and earthquakes in various places" (Matthew 24:6, 7).

Jesus looked into the future from His day and foresaw the crisis of the last generation. For decades the world lived in constant fear of nuclear holocaust as the world's superpowers stockpiled weapons. With the end of the cold war, the world now trembles at the thought of weapons of mass destruction—be they nuclear, biological, or chemical—falling into the hands of fanatical terrorists or rogue nations. Think of Bosnia, of the tribal wars of Africa, of Afghanistan, Iraq, and North Korea, as well as the danger of war that hangs constantly over the entire Middle East.

THE WORLD IS TERRIFIED THAT ROGUE NATIONS WILL OBTAIN NUCLEAR WEAPONS.

PHOTODISC

The restless, strained relations between nations indicate that

Christ, indeed, accurately foretold our day. Yet He also declared, "See to it that you are not alarmed. Such things must happen, but the end is still to come" (verse 6).

Human history has been one of almost constant warfare. While isolated wars do not constitute any particular sign of the end of the world, today war has become so commonplace and so widespread that we often take it for granted.

The demise of the Soviet Union has not increased global security. Actually, there is less. In August of 1999 the television program *60 Minutes II* aired a broadcast revealing that between 1940 and 1960 the Soviet Union recruited thousands of people from all over the nation to live in at least 40 secret cities. Such cities were closed off from the rest of the world—self-contained and heavily guarded. For years the residents received the best food, clothing, and housing. While conditions throughout the Soviet Union were grim, the residents of the secret cities lived like royalty.

What these people did inside the Soviet Union's secret cities has been called "the biggest threat to our national security today." Even while the U.S. downsized nuclear weapons, the Russian secret cities continued to produce plutonium, the key ingredient in most nuclear weapons. During the past 40 years the factories in one city alone produced 40 tons of plutonium, enough for more than 10,000 nuclear bombs.

One Siberian city generated enough plutonium to make a nuclear bomb every three days. And this city, we are told, exists 600 feet underneath a mountain so that if a nuclear attack destroyed everything else, it would still survive to make more nuclear weapons.

But that's not the scary part. Since the Soviet Union collapsed, Russia has gone through some trying economic times. As a result, the workers in those former secret cities have not always been paid on a regular basis, sometimes going for months without regular income. Angry and feeling betrayed, they have been most of all hungry. Attempting to take advantage of the situation, terrorists and rogue governments have come to Russia seeking to buy plutonium to produce nuclear weapons.

In the September/October 1998 issue of the *Bulletin of the Atomic*

Scientists five researchers reported about the threat such nuclear installations pose. "Nothing the United States does to build improved security systems for fissile material is likely to be enough if workers . . . and the guards . . . continue to go unpaid for months at a time, and the economies of the nuclear cities continue to collapse around them."

If we did not have the hope of the Bible—the hope that Jesus will come again soon—these would be scary times indeed.

Notice how Revelation puts it: "The nations were angry; and your wrath has come. The time has come for judging the dead, and for rewarding your servants the prophets and your saints and those who reverence your name, both small and great—and for destroying those who destroy the earth" (Revelation 11:18).

Jesus will return at a time when the human race has the capacity to annihilate itself. With unchecked nuclear weapons, we now have the potential for self-destruction. Certainly this is one of the greatest signs of the coming of Christ.

Broadcasting from Hiroshima in 1945 after the dropping of the atomic bomb, William Ripley stated, "I am standing on the place where the end of the world began." What would he say today—at a time of unprecedented nuclear proliferation?

Jesus pointed forward to our day when He spoke about "men's hearts failing them for fear, and for looking after those things which are coming on the earth: for the powers of heaven shall be shaken" (Luke 21:26, KJV).

CALAMITIES AND DISASTERS

A third sign of the end mentioned by Jesus in Matthew 24 relates to the calamities and disasters so prevalent in modern society: "There will be famines and earthquakes in various places" (Matthew 24:7).

Chaos and disasters vie for the headlines of today's newspapers. Famine causes millions to starve in Africa and other areas of the world. The United Nations recently reported that 15 countries were facing unfavorable prospects for their current crops, while a total of 38 countries anticipated shortfalls in food supplies that would require emergency food

assistance. Experts estimate that for 2 billion people in the world today—nearly one third of the world's population—chronic hunger is an ever-present part of daily life. Twenty-five thousand people a day, or more than 9 million people per year, die of hunger.

IMMENSE STORMS INCREASINGLY DEVASTATE HEAVILY POPULATED AREAS OF THE EARTH.

But even well-fed nations have not escaped the dire predictions of Matthew. "There shall be famines, and pestilences," Jesus said in Matthew 24:7 (KJV). Pestilences are diseases that devastate crops or that run rampant among human beings. They can result from natural causes or be triggered by the carelessness of human beings.

PHOTODISC

PHOTODISC

UNUSUAL WEATHER PATTERNS SHOUT THAT SOMETHING OUT OF THE ORDINARY IS GOING ON.

Today all kinds of scourges afflict herds and crops, seriously affecting the food chain and necessitating the use of chemical-laden sprays and antibiotics to limit them. When someone recently asked a farmer, "How many times do you spray your apples?" he responded, "Twelve to 15 times to produce one crop. Pests are so bad that the apples would be inedible otherwise." Insects are developing immunities to deadly pesticide poisons.

Disease today affects not only the plants in our world, but the human population as well. Cancer, with approximately 100 different strains, is spreading like an epidemic, destroying infants as well as the aged. In addition, society mourns the loss of hundreds of thousands from other diseases unknown only a few years ago.

The Centers for Disease Control and Prevention reports that American industry emits more than 2.4 billion pounds of toxic pollutants into the atmosphere each year and that an estimated 50,000 to 120,000 premature deaths are associated with exposure to air pollutants.

Jesus also predicted frequent earthquakes in the last days. Today we have more than 4,000 seismograph stations in the world that record

12,000 to 14,000 earthquakes per year—that's approximately 35 per day.

Some recent earthquakes that caused significant loss of life are listed here by their location, date, magnitude, and approximate number killed:

Kansu, China; December 16, 1920; 8.6; 180,000
Tangshan, China; July 28, 1976; 7.6; 250,000
Yokohama, Japan; September 1, 1923; 8.3; 140,000
northern Peru; May 31, 1970; 7.7; 70,000
Valparaiso, Chile; August 16, 1906; 8.6; 20,000
Chillan, Chile; January 24, 1939; 8.3; 28,000
northwest Iran; June 20, 1990; 7.3 to 7.7; 40,000
northeast Iran; September 16, 1978; 7.7; 25,000
northern Iran; May 10, 1997; 7.3; 2,400
northwest Armenia; December 7, 1988; 6.9; 25,000
Guatemala; February 4, 1976; 7.5; 22,000
central Mexico; September 19, 1985; 8.1; more than 9,500
northern Afghanistan; May 30, 1998; 6.9; 5,000

All of nature seems to be out of control. A horrible tsunami destroys hundreds of cities and takes between 200,000 and 300,000 lives in India, Sri Lanka, Indonesia, and the islands of the seas. Nature's storms and other unusual weather patterns shout at us that something out of the ordinary is going on.

The list of natural disasters goes on and on, reminding us of Jesus' words: "Men's hearts failing them for fear, and for looking after those things which are coming on the earth" (Luke 21:26, KJV). Such events are harbingers of the coming of the Lord.

A DANGEROUS WORLD

Violence is sweeping our world. Terrorist attacks in Indonesia, Spain, England, Saudi Arabia, Afghanistan, Iraq, Russia, and the United States have changed the face of our world. Fear grips millions. Places that you once felt secure in are gone forever. Crime is up, and lawless elements behave more boldly than ever.

Paul was right when he predicted that "there will be terrible times in the last days" (2 Timothy 3:1). Jesus adds: "iniquity shall abound" (Matthew 24:12, KJV).

By the time a child in North America reaches 12 they've witnessed 2,000 murders on television and more than 100,000 other violent acts. Between November 1996 and November 1998, for example, the Parents' Television Council reported that violence on prime-time television increased 5 percent, foul language 30 percent, and sexual content 42 percent. The situation has only worsened since then. No wonder our moral values are decaying! Children mimic what they see—and so do adults, for that matter.

The Bible's description of the people of Noah's generation reveals their unconcern, their apathy, their total absorption in the things of everyday life (Genesis 6:1-7; Matthew 24:37, 38). When they rejected Noah's warning about the impending Flood, they sealed their own fate. Men and women have not changed with the passing of the centuries. We still lose ourselves in the countless distractions of our day. As a result, we may hear only faintly God's call to us. And while false christs and false prophets arise all around us; while war and rumors of wars rumble; and while earthquakes, scourges, and famines destroy, we fail to discern the signs of the return of Jesus. The world today is as tuned out as was Noah's generation.

SIGNS IN THE WORLD OF KNOWLEDGE

Every time you boot up your computer you might think of a prophecy in Daniel: "But thou, O Daniel, shut up the words, and seal the book, even to the time of the end: many shall run to and fro, and knowledge shall be increased" (Daniel 12:4, KJV). Both knowledge about the prophecies of Daniel and knowledge in general would grow.

And time has proved the truth of that prediction.

Astronomers know more about what's above us, geologists more about what's beneath us, and biologists more about what's within us. Physicians perform delicate surgeries today that medical science didn't even dream of a decade ago. Some have estimated that 80 percent of all the scientists who have ever lived are alive today. The scientific material they produce every 24 hours would take one person a lifetime to read.

PHOTODISC

Some people reading this page may even remember traveling by horse and buggy. Yet they have lived to see the first person walk on the moon and all kinds of space shuttles launched into orbit. They've gone from fountain pens to e-mail and from party-line telephone systems to cell phones the size of their palm.

In the world of computers technology is exploding so rapidly that by the time the common people, like me, figure out how to use their computers, the technology in them is already outdated.

And not only is knowledge increasing exponentially; its accessibility is phenomenal. If you wanted to know something years ago, you had to go to a public library and spend hours in research, or had to visit a special medical, legal, or other type of research center. But today knowledge is accessible at the click of a button—a mouse button. Anything you want to know? Boot up your computer, log on to the Internet, and it's there.

In 1988 approximately 33,000 Internet host sites existed. By 2001 it had increased to 110,000. During a four-year time period from December 1994 to December 1998 America Online subscribers increased from 1.5 million to 15 million, and even these figures are now long obsolete. Tens of millions subscribe to Internet systems.

IN THE LAST DAYS THE PROGRESS OF KNOWLEDGE WILL INCREASE FASTER AND FASTER.

So tomorrow morning when you log on to your computer, remember—that mouse button points to the hope we have in Jesus' soon return.

But Daniel's prophecy—"and knowledge shall be increased"—speaks especially of an understanding of God's Word, the truth about Jesus and His soon return. The Bible predicts a powerful worldwide spiritual revival before the Second Advent: "And this gospel of the kingdom will be preached in the whole world as a testimony to all nations, and then the end will come" (Matthew 24:14).

The aged apostle John, writing from a barren, rocky island in the Aegean Sea, adds: "Then I saw another angel flying in midair, and he had the eternal gospel to proclaim to those who live on the earth—to every nation, tribe, language and people" (Revelation 14:6).

It is a remarkable prediction. Before the return of Jesus, unprecedented doors of opportunity for the proclamation of the gospel will open around the world. Totalitarian regimes will crumble, and oppressive governments will collapse. Miraculously tens of thousands will hear God's Word. I have seen these prophecies fulfilled before my eyes.

Imagine Russian Army trucks delivering 20,000 Bibles to the Kremlin's Congress Hall—the palace of atheism—for thousands to study God's Word. Other thousands have gathered in Moscow's Olympic Stadium to eagerly listen to the gospel. Even more thousands have assembled in auditoriums dedicated to the leaders of atheism throughout the former Communist countries of Poland, Hungary, Yugoslavia, and Romania to hear the preaching of God's Word.

THE PROPHETIC SIGNS OF JESUS' SOON RETURN ARE BEING FULFILLED ALL AROUND US.

Or consider a series of meetings on Bible prophecy sent via satellite throughout Eastern Europe from the former Congress Hall of Communism in Bucharest, Romania, to more than 200,000 people. Through satellite technology and other twenty-first-century communication methods, Christians are communicating the gospel to the ends of the earth. From the Ukraine a satellite series broadcast the story of God's love over the communication systems established by atheists to all 11 time zones of the former Soviet Union.

Through the Internet and laptop computers, God's Word is leaping across geographical boundaries. It is penetrating otherwise unenterable countries, reaching places where hostile elements have tried to keep it out for years.

A spiritual revival has broken out in Africa. Millions of Africans are forsaking tribal religions and coming to Jesus. Throughout Kenya, Ghana, Zambia, and even the Sudan they flock to Christian meetings by the tens of thousands. It's also happening in Central and South America. Through radio, television, Christians witnessing to their neighbors one-on-one, and public meetings in huge stadiums, God's Spirit is moving hearts. In India hundreds of thousands of former Hindus, sometimes even entire villages, are accepting Christ. And in Cambodia, Bangladesh, the Philippines, and Korea God is at work in a special way.

The Spirit is on the move throughout the vast Communist nation of China. Christian faith is undergoing a powerful resurgence. One northern Chinese province, for example, has a Christian congregation with more than 10,000 members. Five hundred people were baptized recently in one small south China community.

From the islands of the sea to massive metropolitan cities, and from poverty-stricken hovels to multimillion-dollar mansions, God is on the move. The prophetic signs of Jesus' soon return are being fulfilled all around us.

CHAPTER 6

REVELATION'S MOST AMAZING PROPHECY

On November 14, 1969, 36 and a half seconds after the Saturn V rocket carrying *Apollo 12* had lifted off the launchpad, lightning struck it. Absurdly, just 15.5 seconds later, lightning hit once again. Virtually every circuit breaker in the command module tripped. Charles (Pete) Conrad, Jr., commander, later reported, "I was aware of a white light. . . . The next thing I noted was that I heard the master alarm ringing in my ears, and I glanced over to the caution and warning panel, and it was a sight to behold." You see, nearly every warning light for the electrical system was on!

Conrad told the people at mission control: We just lost the [stabilizing] platform, gang: I don't know what happened here; we had everything in the world drop out."

John Aaron, a flight controller who supervised the electrical system, looked at his monitor and saw that it no longer displayed any telemetry data. But he knew what to do. He instructed Conrad, "Flight, try SCE to Aux."

While Conrad had no idea what the flight controller was talking about, Alan Bean, the lunar module pilot, knew. Quickly he found the right switch, and immediately Aaron's monitor showed the telemetry data. He had restored power for the *Apollo 12* mission, and four days later, November 18, the lunar module *Intrepid* made a spectacular pinpoint landing in the Ocean of Storms on the moon.

What if the *Apollo 12* astronauts had neglected the urgent message of the alarm lights? What if they had said to themselves "What differ-

PHOTODISC

AFTER MAKING A MIDCOURSE CORRECTION, *APOLLO 12* WENT ON TO LAND ON THE MOON.

ence does it make?" They would have ignored the warning to their own peril.

The alarm lights on the instrument panel of earth are also flashing. We too are aboard a spaceship, one hurtling 828,000 miles an hour toward the constellation Leo. As its passengers, we find ourselves rushing headlong toward an impact with the end-time—speeding toward a collision with the final events of earth's history. Wars and rumors of wars keep disturbing us. Devastating earthquakes make the headlines. The social fabric is falling apart. Violent crime is on the rise. Immorality is commonplace. And the gospel is going to all the world, sweeping through whole countries that once shut it out. All these things are signs that history is reaching a climax.

The blazing alarm lights worry many of the world's leading thinkers. Politicians, scientists, philosophers, sociologists, and a host of others wonder what will happen next. Where is our world headed? Is there some way to realign our moral guidance system? Where can we find direction and stability for the future?

But God knows that the human race is spinning rapidly toward its date with eternity. He knows that the destiny of millions will soon be decided forever. And so, even as events appear to spin out of control, He's devised a solution.

The book of Revelation describes God's midair rescue. "Then I saw another angel flying in midair, and he had the eternal gospel to proclaim to those who live on the earth—to every nation, tribe, language and people" (Revelation 14:6). Wanting to save every person on Planet Earth, the Lord sends a heavenly messenger flying in midair, coming to our rescue. Throughout Revelation John pictures angels as bearing messages from heaven to earth. The fact that one of them bears this message highlights its urgency.

This angel is the first of three who proclaim God's final messages. They represent words of hope sent by a loving God to His people as they stand on the edge of eternity. He has always sent messages to warn His people of approaching events that would affect millions. What happened before the Flood? Did the heavens just pour down rain without warning? No. Noah, in fact, preached for 120 years (Genesis 6:3). Warning that a flood was coming that would destroy life on the earth, he pleaded with people to take refuge in his ark.

God did a similar thing before the great Egyptian famine, sending a messenger to prepare the nation's people. He revealed to Joseph in a dream what was coming. Joseph then had the Egyptians stockpile supplies to meet the famine (Genesis 41).

REVELATION IS AN OPEN BOOK	
1	The Greek word for Revelation is *Apokalypsis,* which literally means "taking away the veil."
2	Revelation takes away the veil regarding the future. It both reveals God's plans and unmasks Satan's.
3	Revelation 1:1 describes the book as "the revelation of Jesus Christ." It is Jesus' own end-time message.
4	In Revelation 22:10 the angel instructs John, "Do not seal up the words of the prophecy of this book, because the time is near."

HISTORY-SHATTERING EVENT

The Lord doesn't play games with humanity. He's not out to catch us off guard; He wants us to be prepared for what is coming. As the prophet Amos put it: "Surely the Sovereign Lord does nothing without revealing his plan to his servants the prophets" (Amos 3:7).

In the book of Revelation God sends a message through His angels that an event of cataclysmic proportions is just over the horizon. It is as if God is announcing, "Something big is coming. But you don't have to be afraid. I will be with you and will provide you with a way of escape. Keep your eyes on Me, and I will tell you what to do."

So what is the big event that God wants us to focus on? If you look at Revelation 14 carefully, you will see something extremely important in verse 14. The Son of Man appears sitting on a cloud. He wears a golden crown on His head and holds a sharp sickle in His hand. "The harvest of the earth is ripe," an angel declares (verse 15). It is the Second Coming—the final judgment when history climaxes and all human destinies are sealed.

THE GOOD NEWS OF WHAT JESUS HAS DONE FOR US IS TO GO TO THE WHOLE WORLD.

So obviously the messages that occur right before this are vitally important. They are God's last warning, His final appeal. He's telling us exactly how to readjust our priorities as we rush toward the end of time.

Let's take a look at the first angel. "Then I saw another angel flying in midair, and he had the eternal gospel to proclaim to those who live on the earth—to every nation, tribe, language and people" (verse 6).

Did you notice the significance of his message? It is a universal one for the entire world. Not an American, African, European, or Asian message, it speaks to all humanity. Leaping across geographical boundaries and breaking down ethnic barriers, it is God's urgent end-time proclamation for the whole world.

The message begins with an angel having "the eternal [everlasting] gospel" to preach. The gospel doesn't change. The good news that saved Paul is the same good news that will redeem the last person on earth. Only one thing can ever rescue sinful human beings—the salvation that Jesus provides in love. We must understand what the three angels say within the context of the gospel. Forces unleashed at the end of time will try to distort and compromise the gospel. That's what the angels warn us about.

WHAT IS THE ETERNAL GOSPEL?

Both panic and lethargy are real dangers as we approach the end. Either can prevent us from grasping the gospel. So let's try to identify this "eternal gospel" as clearly as we can from the words of Scripture.

When the apostle Paul wanted to define the gospel he preached, he summed it up this way: "Christ died for our sins according to the Scriptures, . . . he was buried, . . . he was raised on the third day according to the Scriptures" (1 Corinthians 15:3, 4).

The everlasting gospel, as outlined here, contains four key elements.

First, Jesus Christ died for our sins. He, our Creator, a sinless being, voluntarily marched down that bloody road to Golgotha. Placing his wrists on the cross, He allowed Roman soldiers to pound spikes into His limbs—and He did it on our behalf. Christ voluntarily took the penalty of sin so that we wouldn't have to. The most well-known verse in the Bible puts it beautifully: "For God so loved the world, that he gave his only begotten Son, that whoever believeth in him should not perish, but have everlasting life" (John 3:16, KJV).

The essence of the gospel is that Christ died for our sins. His death was for *us*.

JESUS CONQUERED DEATH, WHICH GIVES US THE HOPE OF ETERNAL LIFE.

HARRY ANDERSON

Second, at the cross Christ laid down His perfect life as a substitute for our sinful life. God credits His righteousness to us, forgiving and accepting us in Jesus Christ. *We* can enter heaven because of the welcome that *He* receives.

Third, Christ rose from the dead. Emerging from the ordeal of the cross victorious, He triumphed over the forces of evil. Three days after His followers took His broken body down from the cross, He arose. An angel rolled the stone away from His tomb and He walked out.

Fourth, Jesus' tomb is empty. Christ has ascended to the Father. His entire interest before the throne of God is to save us as He presents His sacrifice on our behalf before the entire universe. His Spirit convicts us of sin, leads us to repentance, and empowers us to live transformed, godly lives.

The most important question you will ever face in your life is this one—What must I do to be saved? The cross gives a clear answer to it. It restores our broken relationship with God. Jesus didn't die on the cross simply to help us feel better. He sacrificed Himself because we are doomed. Our sins separate us from the life-giving God. Christ gave Himself up on the cross in order to rescue us from eternal death, the inevitable result of sin. We are sinners, responsible before God for what we do and what we become.

If we just keep saying to ourselves, "I'm OK, everything's fine; I'm not any worse than most other people," we will never recognize our true condition. If we don't understand our sinfulness, our self-centeredness, we won't recognize our urgent need for rescue. We won't see the day of final judgment rushing toward us. So the three angels fly through the mid-heavens, declaring God's final message to all humanity. God appeals to us to listen to the warning and let it transform our lives.

A SPECIAL ANGEL'S MESSAGE

That's the backdrop for this message of the first angel in Revelation 14. He proclaims in a loud voice, "Fear God and give him glory, because the hour of his judgment has come. Worship him who made the heavens, the earth, the sea and the springs of water" (Revelation 14:7).

The message has three parts:

- First, it tells us *what* we're supposed to be doing.
- Second, it tells us *why* we are supposed to do it.
- Third, it tells us *when* we are supposed to do it.

First, let's look at what He wants us to be doing. The message tells us to fear God and give glory to Him. What does it mean to fear God? If a messenger from heaven declares that it is something that the Lord expects of us, we'd better find out what it is.

To fear God means to stand in awe of Him. And to be in awe is to deeply admire, revere, and respect. If we respect others, we long to please or obey them. Throughout the Bible, Scripture links together fearing God (or respecting Him) and obeying Him.

THROUGH THE SYMBOLISM OF THE THREE ANGELS SCRIPTURE TELLS US THAT THE GOSPEL WILL GO TO THE WHOLE WORLD.

HARRY ANDERSON

Solomon said: "Here is the conclusion of the matter: Fear God and keep his commandments, for this is the whole duty of man" (Ecclesiastes 12:13). "My son, do not forget my teaching, but keep my commands in your heart. . . . Fear the Lord and shun evil" (Proverbs 3:1-7).

God's last-day message is an urgent call to obey Him at a time in earth's history when millions have the idea that they are responsible only to their own inner sense of right. Today the common belief is: "I can do whatever I choose—I am accountable only to myself. No standard of right or wrong exists outside of my own mind."

The book of Revelation gives us an urgent call: "Fear God"—that is, obey God. There *is* a standard outside of ourselves. The wisest man who ever lived puts it this way: "He who trusts in himself is a fool" (Proverbs 28:26). Revelation's first end-time message appeals to us to seek God's ways, not our own. It calls us to obey Him, not the dictates of our fallen, sinful nature. God's grace leads us not to disobedience but to obedience. Love prompts us not to rebel against God's law but rather to keep it.

John puts this into sharp focus when he writes about "the saints who obey God's commandments and remain faithful to Jesus" (Revelation 14:12).

"Give [God] glory" (verse 7), John the revelator continues. What does that mean?

REVELATION REVEALS AN OUTLINE OF FINAL EVENTS	
1	Jesus' final end-time message will be proclaimed.
2	Millions will respond to it.
3	Millions will reject it.
4	Religion and state will unite at a time of incredible crisis.
5	The mark of the beast will be enforced.
6	An economic boycott and death decree will be passed into law.
7	God's people will face persecution.
8	Every human being will have an opportunity to accept or reject God's love and truth.
9	Human probation will close. God will pour out the seven last plagues during the time of tribulation.
10	Our Lord will return in blazing glory.

Giving God glory means honoring God in everything we do. "Glory" is a word reserved for the highest form of adoration. To give God glory means that we have surrendered our entire lifestyle to reflecting His will for us.

Paul clarifies what it means to glorify God: "You were bought at a price. Therefore honor [glorify] God with your body" (1 Corinthians 6:20). "So whether you eat or drink or whatever you do, do it all for the glory of God" (1 Corinthians 10:31).

Here is a powerful concept: glorify God in all that you do. Everything we do either honors or dishonors Him. For example, we do not give God glory by filling our bodies with destructive substances. Nor do we glorify Him by polluting our minds with this world's filth. Instead, we glorify God by saying, "Lord, my body is Yours. My mind is Yours."

Now to the second part of the first angel's message. The angel tells us the why (the basis) for all obedience—the motivation behind *why* we should fear and glorify God. The Bible repeatedly summons humanity to worship Him because He's the Creator. Here the angel declares, "Worship him who made the heavens, the earth, the sea and the springs of water" (Revelation 14:7).

God created everything—from what we can see through the Hubble telescope to the world we catch a glimpse of in the most powerful electron microscope—and all the mind-boggling complexity of life in between and beyond. He spoke, and from nothingness the universe and its life sprang into being.

WHATEVER WE DO WE SHOULD DO IT IN A WAY THAT HONORS GOD.

We worship God because He created us. John says: "You are worthy, our Lord and God, to receive glory and honor and power, for you created all things, and by your will they were created and have their being" (Revelation 4:11).

Earth's final conflict—its last spiritual war—will center on the issue of worship. Revelation 14:7 summons us to worship the Creator. Verse 9 warns us to avoid worshipping the beast. And verse 12 explains that this final conflict over worship centers on God's commandments.

THE MOST IMPORTANT JUDGMENT OF HISTORY

The third part of the first angel's message explains what makes our allegiance—our worship—so critical. The angel proclaims that the hour of God's judgment has come.

Many people shy away from the idea of a divine judgment, believing that it's pretty scary to stand before God to give account of what they have done. Some even feel that it contradicts the idea of a loving, accepting God. He just forgives with no need to sort things out in a judgment.

But let's step back a moment and get a broader perspective on this subject. Notice the very first verse in the book of Revelation: "The revelation of Jesus Christ, which God gave him to show his servants what must soon take place" (Revelation 1:1).

JESUS IS OUR DEFENDER IN THE FINAL JUDGMENT.

So whom is the book revealing? Jesus Christ. If you want to get to know Jesus, read the Gospels. But don't stop there if you want the whole picture. The book of Revelation is a revelation of Jesus too. It shows us Him deeply involved in end-time judgment. But that judgment also involves the gospel of Jesus, the good news of His salvation. We need to understand that.

CLYDE PROVONSHA

The truth of the gospel does not remove the truth of the judgment. And what is this judgment all about, anyway? Remember that at the beginning of time a rebel angel challenged God's character. Lucifer claimed before the whole universe that God was unfair and unjust. Now, after the passage of thousands of years, the watching universe has seen the results of Satan's activities on our planet. It has witnessed the cruelty, the suffering, the abuse, the horrors of war. It has also observed all the things that God has done to warn people about the results of sin, all the things that He has done to save us.

But some big questions still remain. Has God been fair in His dealings with every individual? Has everyone truly had a chance to make a decision about eternity? Do we really have freedom of choice?

The judgment answers those questions. Because of the judgment and its review of each case, the entire universe gets an opportunity to confirm that God has indeed been fair and just. Everyone can see that the lost have nothing to blame except their own choices. God has done everything He can to save them. At the end of time the whole universe will joyfully proclaim in one chorus of praise: "True and just are his judgments" (Revelation 19:2).

The judgment also deals with sin once and for all. God has to draw a line at some point and say, "Enough!" He doesn't want sin and suffering to go on forever. And so He has appointed a time when the door will slam shut on wickedness, a moment when sin ends. But He will allow everyone to see exactly how He's reached His decisions.

Revelation 14:7 announces that "the hour of his [God's] judgment has come." Verse 14 pictures the arrival of the Son of Man in the clouds, an event that happens *after* the judgment. God's judgment hour thus *precedes* the return of Jesus. Then, based on the results of that judgment, Jesus will "give to everyone according to what he has done" (Revelation 22:12).

If Jesus is coming to give to all their just reward, a judgment must precede His second advent to determine who will receive what. A day will soon come when the choices we have made will forever settle our destiny. John describes it this way: "Let him who does wrong continue to do wrong; let him who is vile continue to be vile; let him who does right continue to do right; and let him who is holy continue to be holy" (Revelation 22:11).

Sin is a deadly disease let loose on our planet. God will eradicate it. But He will do that only at the point when every person has made a decision, when people have chosen between allegiance to Satan and allegiance to God. The goal of Jesus' return is not to destroy sinners, but to erase sin. That's why He has given us this urgent message about His judgment, worship, and allegiance. As we speed toward the final events of earth's history, the judgment is upon us. And too many have let themselves be lulled into a false sense of security. Others see no need for divine forgiveness at all.

AS WE SPEED TOWARD THE FINAL EVENTS OF EARTH'S HISTORY, THE JUDGMENT IS UPON US.

Many years ago in an American frontier town a young man shot and killed a friend in a fit of rage. The act was totally out of character. The fellow had no previous criminal record. An upstanding citizen in the community, he was well liked throughout the county.

The judge in the case sentenced him to death by hanging. Shocked, his family and friends circulated a petition throughout the state. Thousands of people signed it. They appealed to the governor to pardon the young man.

The public response touched the governor's heart. After giving the case considerable thought, he decided to pardon the young man. But to test his sincerity, the governor planned to visit him personally with the pardon. Disguised as a clergyman, the official proceeded to the prison with the document in hand. The prisoner, however, refused to see him. The warden urged the young man to allow at least a brief visit, but he

CLYDE PROVONSHA

vehemently refused. Why should he see any clergyman? He had no time for religion.

A couple hours later the warden visited the prisoner and shared with him the fact that the governor had come with a pardon. Deeply disappointed, the young man wrote the governor a letter of apology. The official simply scrawled across the top of the letter, "No longer interested in this case."

When the authorities were about to hang the prisoner, someone asked him, "Do you have anything to say?" His response was brief but telling. "I am not being hanged for my crime. The governor pardoned it. I am being hanged because I refused the pardon."

GOD APPEALS TO US TO WORSHIP HIM AS CREATOR, SAVIOR, AND LORD.

The man died when he could have lived. He refused the offer of pardon. God has sent an urgent message of His amazing love to the entire human race. To accept it means life, but to reject it leads to eternal death. God respects our freedom of choice. He will not coerce, force, or manipulate anyone. In tones of tenderest love He appeals to each one of us to respond to His grace, to surrender our lives fully to Him, to worship Him as Creator, Savior, and Lord.

Do you sense that He is calling you to a deeper spiritual experience?

CHAPTER 7
THE LONGEST BIBLE PROPHECY

Suppose you take 10 pennies and mark them 1 through 10. Then you place them in your pocket and shake them up. Now try to pull them out in sequence from 1 to 10, returning each coin back in your pocket after each draw.

Your chance of coming up with number 1 is 1 in 10. Drawing numbers 1 and 2 in succession has odds of 1 in 100. And your chance of pulling out numbers 1, 2, and 3 in succession would be 1 in 1,000. Now consider this: your chance of getting 1 through 10 in succession would reach the unbelievable figure of 1 chance in 10 billion.

The odds of drawing the correct order of pennies is staggering. But what about the possibility of predicting with uncanny accuracy dates in the life of Jesus? What if the Bible actually foretold the time of His baptism, His death, and when the gospel would go to the Gentiles?

More amazingly still, what if it formed part of a longer time prophecy predicting when the end-time would begin? And what if it actually revealed the opening of God's great final judgment? This is much more important than counting pennies. It has eternal consequences at stake.

The prophecies of the books of Daniel and Revelation blend to share incredible details regarding the time line of history. They reveal events relating to Jesus' arrival the first time and what will happen before His return.

As we have seen in previous chapters, in Revelation 14:7 John pictures an angel exclaiming with "a loud voice . . . the hour of his [God's] judgment has come." When Jesus returns, the rewards He will give to each person will be with Him, and He will "give to everyone according to what he has done" (Revelation 22:12). The Master clarified this point for His own disciples in Matthew 16:27: "For the Son of Man is going to come in his Father's glory with his angels, and then he will reward each person according to what he has done." As we saw in the previous chapter, a judgment must first take place in heaven to determine who receives what.

One prophecy, the Bible's longest and most amazing one, helps us pinpoint when the judgment will start and where it occurs. As we study the prophecy we will understand why we are living in the end-time of God's judgment hour. And all this can give us a valuable perspective on how to live our lives.

The book of Revelation contains vivid scenes of the hour of God's judgment. But it doesn't tell us much about its timing. To discover when the judgment begins, we must turn back to the prophetic book of Daniel. Daniel unlocks several mysteries in Revelation. God intended for us to study the two books together.

WHERE THE JUDGMENT TAKES PLACE

Let's look first at *where* the judgment takes place: "As I looked, thrones were set in place, and the Ancient of Days took his seat. His clothing was as white as snow; the hair of his head was white like wool. His throne was flaming with fire, and its wheels were all ablaze. A river of fire was flowing, coming out from before him. Thousands upon thousands attended him; ten thousand times ten thousand stood before him. The court was seated, and the books were opened" (Daniel 7:9, 10).

In his dream Daniel found himself in heaven, the throne room of the universe. Tens of thousands of heavenly beings had gathered around God's throne. The supreme court of the universe had begun its final session. The heavenly records revealing God's justice, His fairness, and His incredible love for each individual were now opened. But Daniel 7 ends without revealing the time when the judgment begins. For that we must wait for Daniel 8. The various prophecies of the book of Daniel interlink with each other. Like pieces in a jigsaw puzzle, one piece fits into the next. One chapter of Daniel connects with the next. Daniel 7 begins with four great world empires; Daniel 8 covers much of the same territory. Then the prophet comes to the judgment and declares, "Unto two thousand and three hundred days; then shall the sanctuary be cleansed" (Daniel 8:14, KJV).

What is this cleansing of the sanctuary and how does it relate to God's final judgment? When Daniel wrote these words to his Jewish readers, they knew what he meant. Sanctuary language was very familiar to them. Since the time of Moses, God's people had followed a detailed worship program that centered on their earthly sanctuary service, either in the portable tabernacle or in the Jerusalem Temple. The Lord intended the services of the earthly sanctuary to serve as an illustration of the plan of salvation. God wanted certain truths to stand out clearly. The offering of a lamb without blemish,

THE RITUALS OF THE HEBREW TABERNACLE SYMBOLIZED HOW GOD SAVES HUMAN BEINGS.

UNDERSTANDING TIME PROPHECY

In Bible prophecy one prophetic day equals one literal year.

EZEKIEL 4:6 "I have assigned you . . . a day for each year."

NUMBERS 14:34 "For forty years—one year for each of the forty days . . . —you will suffer for your sins."

for example, pointed forward to the Lamb of God, Jesus Christ, who laid down His sinless life as a sacrifice on our behalf.

The sanctuary had two main rituals—the daily service and the yearly service. In a typical daily service a person who had sinned brought a sacrifice to the Temple. There the individual confessed the sin over the animal, and the animal was killed. A priest caught the blood in a basin, poured most of it out at the base of the altar, then took the rest of it into the sanctuary. In this way the priest symbolically transferred sin from the sinner to the substitute, then to the sanctuary. Again, that innocent slain lamb pointed forward to Christ's ultimate sacrifice on our behalf.

Now, in a sense, this stream of sacrificial blood flowed all year, bringing sin into the sanctuary. And that's why the yearly service was required. On the tenth day of the seventh month of the religious year the Hebrews participated in the Day of Atonement. That's when the sanctuary was cleansed. "This is to be a lasting ordinance for you: On the tenth day of the seventh month you must deny yourselves and not do any work— . . . because on this day atonement will be made for you, to cleanse you. Then, before the Lord, you will be clean from all your sins" (Leviticus 16:29, 30).

Actually, the people's soul-searching began 10 days before the Day of Atonement when trumpet blasts announced the approach of that solemn day. Those who deliberately ignored the warning were shut off from the people. They were judged.

WHEN DID THE JUDGMENT BEGIN?

This cleansing of the sanctuary in the Old Testament illustrated something that would happen before Christ's coming. While the daily sacrifices depicted the sacrifice of Christ, the cleansing of the sanctuary pointed forward to something else. Daniel 8:14 says that after 2,300 days the sanctuary would be cleansed, referring to a judgment that takes place before the end of earth's history. The earthly ceremonies described in Leviticus 16 are shadows of God's judgment in the heavenly sanctuary that will occur just before Jesus comes again.

The sacrificial lamb depicted the coming crucifixion of Christ.

The Old Testament Day of Atonement employed two goats—the goat for the Lord and the goat for Azazel (scapegoat). The priests sacrificed the Lord's goat. The high priest took its blood into the sanctuary and through the veil into the Most Holy Place. He sprinkled the blood before the mercy seat that rested on a chest called the ark of the covenant. The gold-covered box contained the original, divinely etched Ten Commandments. It symbolized God's throne in heaven, where Jesus represents His people today (Hebrews 8-10). The high priest as he came before the mercy seat stood in the very presence of God. He represented Jesus Christ, our heavenly high priest, who now appears before God in heaven on our behalf .

After the sacrifice of the Lord's goat, a specially chosen person led the scapegoat into the wilderness, where it wandered until it died. This represented the death of Satan, the originator of sin. Each year, the sanctuary services reminded the Israelites of the future sacrifice of the Savior and of the final elimination of sin from the universe. Thus each year

Siegfried Bohlman

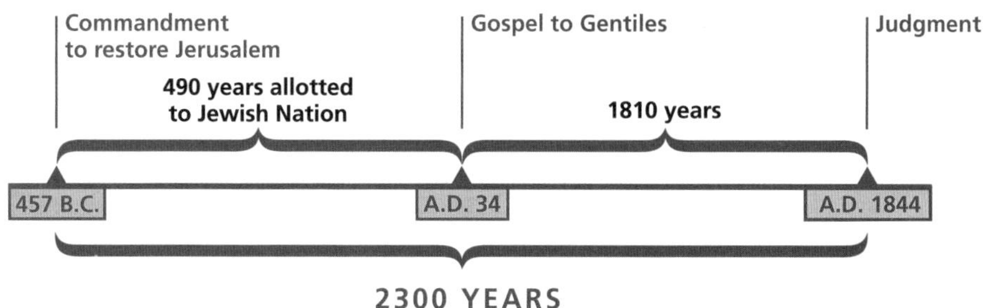

God's people participated in a service that prepared them for His ultimate judgment.

The cleansing of the sanctuary in Daniel 8:14 and its allusion to the Day of Atonement thus refers to a very specific process of judgment. But when did that process begin? Let's look at the time frame of the prophecy. Daniel says that after 2,300 days the sanctuary would be cleansed. (Some versions speak of restoration.)

The prophet himself really didn't know what that meant. His vision perplexed him. But God, being who He is, sent an angel to explain things. "And I heard a man's voice from the Ulai calling, 'Gabriel, tell this man the meaning of the vision.' As he came near the place where I was standing, I was terrified and fell prostrate. 'Son of man,' he said to me, 'understand that the vision concerns the time of the end'" (Daniel 8:16, 17).

Notice three points that we can infer from this passage. They shed light on the 2,300-day prophecy.

First, the vision extends to the close of our world's history—to "the time of the end."

Second, the 2,300 days apply to God's heavenly sanctuary. Why? Because the earthly system of sacrifices, obsolete after the death of Christ, had been fulfilled long before the end of the prophecy.

Third, the 2,300 days represent a time period couched in the symbolic language of apocalyptic prophecy.

We must keep in mind that a day represents a year in Bible prophecy. Ezekiel 4:6, in a symbolic prophecy of punishment for the nation of Israel,

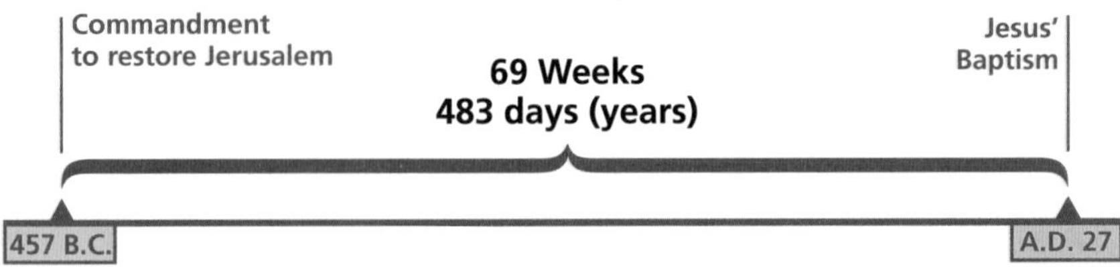

THE WORD "MESSIAH" MEANS "THE ANOINTED ONE."

Jesus began His ministry with the anointing of the Holy Spirit at His baptism (Acts 10:37, 38).

has God telling the prophet, "I have assigned you 40 days, a day for each year." So we can conclude that the 2,300 days represents 2,300 years.

The angel Gabriel explained more to Daniel about the 2,300 days. That time period was divided into two segments. First, he says in Daniel 9:24: "Seventy weeks are determined upon thy people and upon thy holy city" (KJV). The period thus relates to "thy people," the Jews. The 70 weeks equal 490 days, or, in prophecy, 490 years. During this time period the Jews had the opportunity to accomplish the work that God gave them. The Lord would have to use other means to accomplish His purposes if they failed.

THE KEY TO UNLOCKING THE 2,300-DAY PROPHECY CAN BE FOUND IN DANIEL 9:25.

Those 70 weeks—490 years—are "determined," that is, cut off, from the 2,300 days or years. That leaves us with 1,810 years remaining. The remaining 1,810 years would lead to an event called the "cleansing of the sanctuary," or the time of judgment.

Now let's look at the master key for unlocking this entire time prophecy: "Know therefore and understand, that from the going forth of the commandment to restore and to build Jerusalem unto the Messiah the Prince shall be seven weeks, and threescore and two weeks" (Daniel 9:25, KJV). As you know, a score equals 20, so "threescore and two" makes 62.

When Daniel received this prophecy, his people were exiles, captives in Babylon. Jerusalem lay in ruins. The angel told Daniel that this time prophecy would begin with the issuing of an imperial decree that would allow the Jews to return to their homeland and rebuild Jerusalem. Artaxerxes, king of Persia, made that decree in the fall of 457 B.C. So now we have a starting date. The seventy weeks, or 490 years, began in 457 B.C. And the 2,300 days, or years, thus commenced at the same time.

THE BAPTISM AND DEATH OF JESUS PREDICTED

Do you know what we discover if we follow this time line? We find that Daniel foretells the years of the baptism and death of Jesus. It also foretells the time when the gospel would begin to be proclaimed to the Gentile world.

Notice what the prophecy says: There would be 62 weeks plus seven weeks from the decree to restore Jerusalem until the coming of the Messiah. That's a total of 69 prophetic weeks, or 483 literal years. So with these momentous events in mind, let's go back to our starting point, 457 B.C. That's the decree that triggers everything (Ezra 6:14; 7:8-28). Now let's add 483 years to 457 B.C. Remember that in B.C. time we're counting down. It takes us to A.D. 26. But we must also keep in mind that there was no zero year in history. Historians record the shift between the two eras of history as going from 1 B.C. to A.D. 1. So we must add a year to compensate, coming up with A.D. 27.

> JESUS OFTEN PROCLAIMED, "THE TIME IS FULFILLED" (MARK 1:14, 15, KJV).

What happened in A.D. 27? According to many scholars, that's the year that the Messiah, Jesus Christ, the anointed one, began His public ministry following His baptism. It happened in the fall of the year during the fifteenth year of the reign of Tiberius. This remarkable prophecy gives special meaning to what Jesus often proclaimed in His preaching: "The time is fulfilled" (Mark 1:14, 15, KJV). The time had indeed been fulfilled. That 69-week prophecy, given approximately 500 years before the birth of Christ, pointed to the year of Christ's baptism.

Now according to most interpretations of the chronology of the Gospels, the ministry of Christ lasted precisely three and a half years. Guess what? Again Daniel's prophecy predicted it: "And after threescore and two weeks shall Messiah be cut off. . . . And he shall confirm the covenant with many for one week: and in the midst of the week he shall cause the sacrifice and the oblation to cease" (Daniel 9:26, 27, KJV).

The Bible predicted that in the middle of this last week—the seventieth week allotted to the Jewish nation—sacrifices of the earthly sanctuary service would in some way come to an end. Remember that the sixty-ninth week ended in A.D. 27. One last prophetic week remained. In other words, seven years remained. Note that "in the midst of the week" some kind of an end to sacrifice would take place. What's the middle of the prophetic week? Three and a half years. Add three and a half years to A.D. 27 and it brings us to A.D. 31.

Amazingly, at this time, during the feast of Passover in the spring of A.D. 31, Jesus was crucified. The Jewish sacrificial system no longer had any meaning as a foreshadow of His atoning death. Christ, our Passover Lamb, had been sacrificed. During "the midst of the week," the last prophetic week of the period allotted to the Jews, Jesus died as our Redeemer.

What about the end of the week, that is, three and a half more years after A.D. 31? Although the book of Acts does not give any exact date, many scholars believe that the first Christian martyr, Stephen, was stoned to death by the religious leadership at this point. The focus of the church now shifted from just the Jews alone to the world at large. Since the official Temple leadership refused to accept Jesus as Messiah and proclaim Him, the gospel was now free to go to the Gentiles as well. The

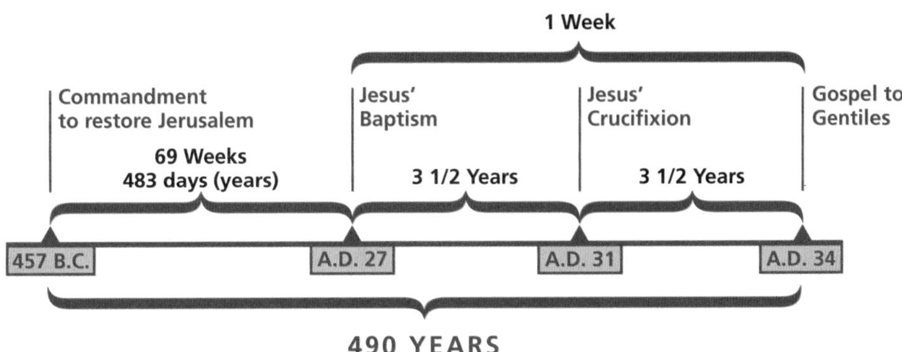

Messiah was no longer exclusive to the Jews. The 70 weeks, or 490 years, allowed to the nation of Israel had now concluded.

Centuries in advance the prophet Daniel had laid all this out—the year of Christ's baptism, the year of His crucifixion, and when preaching the gospel was broadened to include the Gentiles. We have now clearly accounted for the 70 weeks cut off from the 2,300-day prophecy.

LIVING IN GOD'S JUDGMENT HOUR

But what about the remaining time of that prophecy? After we advance 70 weeks, or 490 years, from the starting point, 457 B.C., we still have 1,810 years left. Add them to A.D. 34, and we come to 1844. What did the Bible predict would happen at the end of the 2,300 day/year prophecy? The sanctuary would be cleansed, and judgment would begin at that time.

That's the message that Daniel reveals. It's a solemn thing to consider. Since 1844 we have been living in God's judgment hour. God considers His judgment so important that He pictures an angel flying in the midst of heaven announcing with a loud voice: "Fear God and give him glory, because the hour of his judgment has come" (Revelation 14:7).

The Lord looks over the "books"—the heavenly data banks—that record the deeds of every human being throughout history. The cosmic court reviews names and examines each case. Someday when God completes this awesome task, Christ will descend to earth to claim His own.

We are indeed living during the judgment session, heading toward the climax of history. Do you have confidence today about how that final investigation in heaven will decide your case? Or are you worried about your fate in the judgment hour?

Even if God does carefully weigh all the good and bad in each of our lives, most of us would probably still feel we're on very shaky ground. Only the most misguided egotists would claim that they have earned a spot in God's holy heaven as they in their minds stare up at those thrones of God's supreme court.

Our cases demand more than justice and fairness. We're all guilty when confronted with the standard of God's holy law. And that standard is not going to bend for any of us. Just as the United States Supreme Court justices must uphold the Constitution and apply it consistently, so our sovereign God will uphold His own law.

So what hope is there? If it was just a situation of our good deeds being weighed against our bad deeds, our case might well be hopeless. However, God does not count our good works and then tally up our sins to see which number is greater. Instead, thank God, in the judgment the one factor that makes all the difference is our commitment to Jesus.

The essential question is Have we accepted Jesus Christ as our personal Savior? Our actions must reflect this inner belief. The judgment is not about our being good enough to enter heaven. Rather, it is about Jesus loving us enough to save us. It is about our loving, righteous, compassionate Savior, who poured out His life on Calvary's cross so that not one person need be lost.

Revelation's prophecy proclaims in trumpet tones, "The hour of [God's] judgment has come." We are not the only ones on trial before the universe. God also faces a verdict. Satan, that rebel angel, has claimed that God is unfair and unjust. The judgment reveals that God has done everything He could to redeem every human being. He now opens the heavenly records for the entire universe to see. They reveal His unceasing efforts to save us. Only those who rejected His love, spurned His mercy, and turned their backs on His grace will be lost.

Heaven declares that the hour of God's judgment has come.

James Padgett

I believe that on the day of judgment Christ will say to the Father (and the universe), "Yes, this person is guilty of sin. As is the case of every human being, he or she has fallen short of Your glory. But now he or she has been adopted as Our son or daughter. He or she has accepted My sacrifice for sin on his or her behalf and chosen to ask Our help in overcoming sin. Therefore, I ask that You accept him or her into heaven on the basis of the perfect life I lived on earth."

That is what our Advocate can say on our behalf. He is going to win the case—He's going to win every time.

While God's supreme court is interested in justice—in upholding divine law—it's also focused on something more: the believer's bill of rights. All those who commit their lives to Christ as Lord and Savior receive incredible privileges and rights. Our long record of good and bad deeds will no longer be used against us. Instead, we have the right to call on the righteousness of Christ.

ALL THOSE WHO COMMIT THEIR LIVES TO CHRIST RECEIVE INCREDIBLE PRIVILEGES AND RIGHTS.

Many years ago in Germany a young musician named Friedrich Wilhelm Herschel played in the band of the Hanoverian Guards. His superior talent won him much admiration. But when war came and he had to huddle in trenches as the cannons roared all night, terror overwhelmed the young man. One night the 19-year-old couldn't take any more and fled the battlefield. His father sent him to England, where he became known as William.

There he became a great organist and also began to study astronomy. The years passed. First he rented a telescope and later he was able to build his own. One evening he located what he thought might be a comet. As it turned out, William had discovered the first new planet since antiquity—the planet Uranus. Soon the world was acclaiming his discovery, and on December 7, 1781, he was elected to the Royal Society. The very next year the king of England sent for him.

As William approached Windsor Castle for his appointment, however, a terrible dread, instead of joyous anticipation, filled him, because the king of England's grandfather, George I, had once ruled the kingdom of Hanover. It was that principality whose army William had served in. George III would recognize William as a deserter.

As he sat in an antechamber, waiting for his audience with the king, a servant approached and presented William with an envelope. With trembling hands he opened it. Would he finally look at his long-awaited condemnation? Instead Herschel found a full and complete pardon for his act of desertion.

Overjoyed, William was ushered into the presence of the king. The monarch told him, "Now that you are pardoned we can talk freely, and you shall become Sir William Herschel."

When your appointment with the King of the universe comes on that final day of reckoning, you need not tremble with fear. You don't have to worry about some past act of indiscretion, some terrible mistake rising up to condemn you. God has already written out a pardon full and free. All those who have looked up at Jesus Christ, the bright, morning star—all those who have seen Him rise in their hearts as Savior and Lord—will find that He has wiped the past away. Only Christ's grace will stand in that supreme court—only His merits will count. But they are more than enough to win us an eternal home in heaven.

CHAPTER 8

WHEN TRUTH DEMANDS CHANGE

The discovery of new Bible truths always demands change in our lives. The book of Revelation presents the blessings of God not simply for "the one who reads" and those who "hear" its last-day prophecies, but to those who "take to heart" the truth revealed (Revelation 1:3). One of the most profound end-time truths appears in Revelation 14:6 and 7. According to verse 6 the eternal gospel will go to every "nation, tribe, language and people." A universal message for all humanity, it spans oceans and leaps across continents, all the while breaking down ethnic barriers. It is not for simply a single people group; instead, it is a timely, urgent, vital truth for the entire planet.

The heart of God's message is a call to worship the Creator. An angel flying directly from the throne of God revealed it to the exiled apostle John on the Isle of Patmos in these words: "Fear God and give him glory, because the hour of his judgment has come. Worship him who made the heavens, the earth, the sea and the springs of water" (Revelation 14:7). Why do we worship God and give Him praise, honor, and adoration? Simply because He created us. We are not here by chance. Life is not a cosmic accident.

The book of Revelation pictures heavenly beings encircling God's throne singing, "You are worthy, our Lord and God, to receive glory and honor and power, for you created all things, and by your will they were created and have their being" (Revelation 4:11). The very heart of all worship is an acknowledgment of God as Creator.

As we saw previously, Scripture describes a titanic struggle between two forms of worship—worshipping the Creator (Revelation 14:7) and worshipping the beast (verse 9). In reality, this conflict over worship centers on the last battle between Jesus and Satan. To the surprise of many, the Bible teaches that Jesus Christ was God's agent in Creation. The apostle Paul puts it this way: He is "the image of the invisible God. . . . By him all things were created" (Colossians 1:15, 16). In the Epistle to the Ephesians he adds: "And to make all men see what is the fellowship of the mystery, which from the beginning of the world hath been hid in God, who created all things by Jesus Christ" (Ephesians 3:9, KJV). God the Father—the all-wise, all-powerful God—created our world by or through His Son, Jesus Christ.

Satan hates the truth that Jesus is the Creator, because as the evil one he destroys instead of builds up. Since he does not have the power to give life, he takes it. In the end all of us will face one of two choices—worshipping the Creator (the source of life) or worshipping the beast (the origin of death).

EARTH'S FINAL ISSUE OF LOYALTY

Is it possible that Revelation's call to worship the Creator is at the heart of earth's final issue of loyalty to God? Could it be the focus of a truth, long lost sight of, that God will reveal to the end-time generation?

What if you discovered a biblical truth that no one else in the world was following—or at least you thought no one else was? Would you have the courage to do what the Bible says even if the rest of the world paid no attention to it? How long would you persist? Let me tell you an amazing story about a woman who was so profoundly convinced that she had discovered truth that she followed what she saw as the claims of Scripture the rest of her life.

Maria lived in a small Ukrainian village. She had a sincere desire to seek God's truth from the time she was a child. As she prayed and studied the Bible, asking God to reveal His will, she came across the fourth commandment, which emphatically states, "Remember the Sabbath day

OLD TESTAMENT BIBLE PASSAGES ON THE SIGNIFICANCE OF THE SABBATH

Genesis 2:1-3; Exodus 16:23-30;
Exodus 20:8-11; Leviticus 23:3, 38;
Deuteronomy 5:12-15;
2 Chronicles 23:6-8;
Nehemiah 9:14; 10:31; 13:15-22;
Isaiah 56:2-6; 58:13; 66:23;
Jeremiah 17:21-24, 27;
Ezekiel 20:12, 20;
Ezekiel 20:24; 22:26; 46:1; Amos 8:5

by keeping it holy. Six days you shall labor and do all your work, but the seventh day is a Sabbath to the Lord your God" (Exodus 20:8-10). As she continued to pray for wisdom on the subject of the Sabbath, Maria felt deeply impressed that the true biblical day of worship was the seventh day of the week, as the fourth commandment so plainly stated.

Maria began to share her convictions with her friends at church. Not one was interested. In time she did the only thing she believed an honest-hearted Christian could do. She followed her convictions. Believing what the Bible said, she began to observe the Sabbath by herself, a practice she followed for more than 30 years.

A few years ago a Christian book salesman visited her home. When Maria shared her deepest convictions with him, her visitor explained that he too kept the Bible Sabbath. Joy overwhelmed Maria. Now she knew of at least two Sabbathkeepers in the world. To her amazement, he explained that millions more lived in almost every country. They too were observing God's holy day.

Could it be most people are overlooking this vital truth that Maria discovered? Is it possible that the Christian church at large has missed something as important as the Sabbath of the fourth commandment, which God wrote with His own finger on tables of stone? Sabbath symbolizes the creatorship of God, "for in six days the Lord made the heavens and the earth, the sea, and all that is in them, but he rested on the seventh day. Therefore the Lord blessed the Sabbath day and made it holy" (Exodus 20:11).

In an age of evolution, humanism, and godless materialism, maybe God is calling us back to our roots at Creation. The essence of all life is the reality of the fact that God brought us into being. So let us travel back

NEW TESTAMENT BIBLE PASSAGES ON THE SIGNIFICANCE OF THE SABBATH

Matthew 12:2, 12; 24:20;
Mark 1:21; 2:27, 28;
Mark 3:2-4; 6:1, 2; 16:1;
Luke 4:16, 31; 6:1-9; 13:14-16;
14:3-5; 23:45-58;
John 5:9-18; 7:22, 23; 9:14-16;
Acts 13:27, 42-44; 15:21; 18:4;
Hebrews 4:1, 4, 5

to the beginning to uncover the meaning of life today.

We begin our journey with the apostle John, who wrote, "In the beginning was the Word, and the Word was with God, and the Word was God. He was with God in the beginning. Through him all things were made, and without him nothing was made that has been made" (John 1:1-3).

A loving God established our amazing and intricate world. Starting with a shapeless mass of darkness, the Creator dazzled it with light, enveloped it with an atmosphere, salted it with seas, brightened it with plants, and enlivened it with moving creatures. And each day as He completed His work, He looked upon His handiwork and said, "It is good!"

Notice how God finished Creation week. "Thus the heavens and the earth were completed in all their vast array. By the seventh day God had finished the work he had been doing; so on the seventh day he rested from all his work. And God blessed the seventh day and made it holy, because on it he rested from all the work of creating that he had done" (Genesis 2:1-3).

The word "rested" shows up twice in these verses. Did God rest because He was tired? Apparently not, because Isaiah 40:28 says: "Do you not know? Have you not heard? The Lord is the everlasting God, the Creator of the ends of the earth. He will not grow tired or weary."

What does it mean, then, when it says that God rested? It tells us that He was no longer working, because He had finished His task. When I turn off my car engine, I can accurately say that the engine is at rest. It is no longer moving—no longer working.

Now observe with me something else about that word "rested." The book of Genesis was originally written not in English, but in Hebrew. And in Hebrew the word translated into English as "rest" is *shabath.*

Shabath has entered the English language as the word "Sabbath." So "sabbath" and "rest" mean the same thing. Now let's go back to something we looked at earlier in Genesis. "On the seventh day," Genesis 2:2 told us, God "rested from all his work"—that is, He "sabbathed."

A SPECIAL DAY SET ASIDE BY GOD

Our passage in Genesis 2:1-3 tells us that God did three things on the Sabbath. He rested on the seventh day, He blessed the seventh day, and He sanctified the seventh day. Nowhere in Scripture does the Bible indicate that God rested on, blessed, or sanctified any other day. When we rest on the seventh-day Sabbath, we do so on the day God that rested on. When we worship the Creator of heaven and earth on Sabbath, we receive the blessing that God put into the Sabbath but no other day. Human beings cannot set a day apart as holy or truly sanctify a day—only God can. And the seventh day is the one He chose.

For 40 years the gathering of the manna was a weekly reminder of the Sabbath.

God's loyal followers kept the Sabbath that He gave them from Creation down through history to the time of His people Israel. Bible history reveals the sad fact that by the time of Moses God's people, after centuries in Egyptian bondage, had forgotten their roots and His special day of fellowship. But He had a plan to remind His people of His special day. As Moses led the Israelites out of their captivity in Egypt to the

Promised Land, their food supply ran out in the Sinai wilderness. To meet their need, God miraculously provided bread from heaven, called "manna," for 40 years.

The story involves more than just receiving a daily food supply. The manna appeared on the ground only six days a week. God instructed the Israelites to gather enough manna on the sixth day to meet their needs for the seventh day. The manna never fell on the Sabbath, and if anyone collected extra in advance on any day other than the sixth, it would spoil.

Why? God wanted His people to know that the One who led them out of Egypt was also their Creator. Signifying the importance of the seventh day through the way He supplied the manna, the Lord sought to help His people realize that His day had a very special purpose. It had in no way faded in significance with the passing of time.

When God gave Moses the Ten Commandments, they reminded the human race about the Sabbath.

As God led them through the Sinai Peninsula to the Promised Land, He gave them a reminder of the Sabbath through the way He supplied manna. He also found it necessary to restate His Ten Commandments. During their long stay in Egypt the Israelites had forgotten much of what they knew about Him.

Harry Anderson

So the Lord reminded them of His law as they camped at the base of Mount Sinai. And the fourth of those Ten Commandments said: "Remember the Sabbath day by keeping it holy. Six days you shall labor and do all your work, but the seventh day is a Sabbath to the Lord your God. On it you shall not do any work, neither you, nor your son or daughter, nor your manservant or maidservant, nor your animals, nor the alien within your gates. For in six days the Lord made the heavens and the earth, the sea, and all that is in them, but he rested on the seventh day. Therefore the Lord blessed the Sabbath day and made it holy" (Exodus 20:8-11).

Here God commands His people to remember His weekly memorial of Creation—the seventh-day Sabbath. And He promises His people many blessings as they mark this special day each week. Listen to God speaking in Isaiah 58:13 and 14: "If you keep your feet from breaking the Sabbath and from doing as you please on my holy day, if you call the Sabbath a delight and the Lord's holy day honorable, and if you honor it by not going your own way and not doing as you please or speaking idle words, then you will find your joy in the Lord." And millions around the world today can testify to the blessings they enjoy from observing the weekly seventh-day Sabbath.

THE SABBATH BEGAN AT CREATION, BEFORE ANY JEWS EXISTED.

Some people have the idea that God gave the seventh-day Sabbath to only the Israelites at Sinai—that it was an exclusively Jewish day. But we've seen from the book of Genesis that the Sabbath began at Creation—before any Jews ever existed.

Notice too that when God reminded Israel about the Sabbath, He said, "Remember the Sabbath day." It's hard to remember something you've never heard of before. A Bible society handbook on translating the book of Exodus observes that God is here telling His people, "See that you remember to observe" the Sabbath.

According to both Genesis and Exodus, then, what day is the Sabbath? The seventh day, and if you look at most calendars, it is clear that Saturday is the seventh day of the week. That immediately raises a question. If Saturday is the seventh-day Sabbath, why do most Christians go to church on Sunday? Muslims, who also believe in the story of Moses, have chosen Friday as their day for special worship. What's going on here?

Two possibilities are open to us from the Christian perspective:

1. Someone has changed most calendars so that Saturday has replaced Sunday as the seventh day of the week. Or:
2. Someone has changed the Sabbath, or Lord's Day, from Saturday, the seventh day, to Sunday, the first day of the week.

WHICH DAY IS THE SEVENTH DAY?

How can we accurately identify which day the seventh day is? Consider most standard calendars. Sunday is the first day, Saturday the seventh. Although some European calendars begin with Monday as the first day and end with Sunday as the seventh day, throughout the centuries the day in the English-speaking countries that we call Saturday has always been the seventh day. The introduction of Sunday as the seventh day on some European calendars occurred in the 1950s for the convenience of business, since the workweek there begins on Monday. According to such trustworthy sources as the Royal Greenwich Observatory in Greenwich, England, and the United States Naval Observatory, the weekly cycle has never changed.

In more than 140 languages around the world the day called "Saturday" in English is some form of the word "Sabbath." In Spanish and Portuguese, for example, it is *Sabado*, and in Arabic, it is known as *sabit*. Such widespread use clearly demonstrates that the seventh day of the week, Saturday, is the true Sabbath. *Merriam-Webster's Collegiate Dictionary*, eleventh edition, defines Saturday as "the seventh day of the week."

But, some may ask, didn't scholars in the Western world change the calendar to keep the months from drifting from season to season? The older Julian calendars did not take into account that the year is not exactly 365 days, and after a long passage of time, the calendars had gotten out of step with astronomical time. To correct this problem, Pope Gregory XIII decreed in A.D. 1582 that the day following Thursday, October 4, 1582, would be Friday, October 15, 1582. Pope Gregory's adjustment corrected the count, and we've been basically on track ever since.

LANGUAGES OF THE WORLD TESTIFY THAT SATURDAY IS THE SEVENTH DAY

	LANGUAGES	WORD FOR SEVENTH DAY	MEANING
1	Greek	Sabbaton	Sabbath
2	Spanish	Sábado	Sabbath
3	Portuguese	Sabado	Sabbath
4	Italian	Sabato	Sabbath
5	French	samedi	Sabbath
6	German	Samstag	Sabbath
7	Russian	Sabbota	Sabbath
8	Polish	Sobota	Sabbath
9	Hebrew	Shabat	Sabbath
10	Persian	Shambin	Sabbath
11	Hindi	Szombat	Sabbath
12	Arabic	As sabit	Sabbath
13	Malay	Ari-Sabtu	Sabbath
14	Abyssinian	Sanbat	Sabbath

But note something very important here. The change did not disturb the weekly cycle. Friday still followed Thursday, Saturday came after Friday, and Sunday after Saturday. The seventh day of the week was still Saturday, and the first day of the week was still Sunday. Saturday has always been the seventh day.

Well, then, what about that second possibility? Has someone attempted to shift the worship day from Saturday to Sunday? The answer is yes. But it was not God's doing. The Bible knows nothing of a change in the Sabbath.

While still here on earth, Jesus said: "Do not think that I have come to abolish the Law or the Prophets; I have not come to abolish them but to fulfill them" (Matthew 5:17). His teaching about the seventh-day Sabbath is too plain to be misunderstood. He did not come to destroy it, but to fulfill it. To fulfill means to make something full of meaning. Jesus filled the seventh-day Sabbath with meaning. He broke down the nonbiblical Jewish regulations that overshadowed the true spiritual significance of the day and especially discouraged Gentiles from observing it. Jesus gave us a positive example of Sabbathkeeping in His life. The Gospel writer Luke states: "And, as his

THE CALENDAR CHANGE

Authorized by Pope Gregory XIII in February of 1582 and went into effect in October of that year. The dates changed, but the sequence of days did not alter.

OCTOBER 1582

Sunday	Monday	Tuesday	Wednesday	Thursday	Friday	Saturday
	1	2	3	4	15	16
17	18	19	20	21	22	23
24	25	26	27	28	29	30
31						

From Creation the weekly cycle has always remained an unbroken cycle of seven days.

custom was, he went into the synagogue on the sabbath day, and stood up for to read" (Luke 4:16, KJV). Each Sabbath for nearly 30 years the carpenter shop in Jesus' hometown, Nazareth, was empty, His tools neatly put in place. Jesus set aside the Sabbath to worship His heavenly Father. He would not miss heaven's richest blessings each Sabbath.

WHAT DOES IT MEAN TO BE UNDER THE LAW?

- The apostle Paul teaches that we are "not under law, but under grace" (Romans 6:14).
- To be under the law means to be under the law as a method of salvation (Romans 3:19, 20)
- To be under grace means to be under grace as a method of salvation (Ephesians 2:8; Romans 3:28).
- God's grace is our only means of salvation, but grace always leads to obedience, never disobedience (Romans 3:31; 6:15).

Speaking of the destruction of Jerusalem in A.D. 70, Jesus said to His closest followers, "Pray that your flight will not take place in winter or on the Sabbath" (Matthew 24:20). Why would Christ Himself tell the disciples to pray that they would not have to flee Jerusalem on the Sabbath if they were not observing it? If they were worshipping on the first day of the week, it would make no sense at all. But if the early Christians were keeping Sabbath and the Roman armies attacked on the seventh day, it would be much easier for the soldiers to slay them all since they would be together worshipping on the Sabbath.

When Jesus was crucified, the Bible says that He died on Friday, called the Preparation Day. Then He rested in the tomb on Saturday, the Sabbath of the commandment. And finally He was resurrected on Sunday, the first day of the week (Luke 23:52; 24:1).

The closest followers of Christ kept the Bible Sabbath after His death. The apostle Paul not only preached to the Jews about Jesus on Sabbath; he conducted public worship services for the entire city of Antioch on Sabbath. "On the next Sabbath almost the whole city gathered to hear the word of the Lord" (Acts 13:44). The city of Philippi had no organized Jewish or Christian congregation. But that did not stop Paul from honoring the Sabbath. "On the Sabbath we went outside the city gate to the river, where we expected to find a place of prayer. We sat down and began to speak to the women who had gathered there" (Acts 16:13). If Jews did not have enough male believers to establish a synagogue, they would meet in some private place—often at the edge of the city or, in this case, beside a nearby river. The disciples certainly did not change the day God set aside as a memorial to Creation.

To learn how most Christians began worshipping on the first day of the week instead of the Sabbath, we must turn to early church history. And here we discover that in the centuries immediately following the death of Christ's apostles, Christian worship began to focus more on Sunday than on the Sabbath. This came about as a result of both pressures coming from the surrounding cultures and from church and government decrees. The fascinating story of how the shift happened is the subject of our next chapter.

So, you see, even though most Christians today attend church on Sunday and sincerely believe they are worshipping God on the right day, it simply is not the case.

A MEMORIAL OF CREATION

Many people assume that somewhere the New Testament supports a transfer of the Sabbath from Saturday, the seventh day, to Sunday, the first day, as a memorial of Christ's resurrection. Christ has indeed left us a memorial of His resurrection—but it is the ordinance of baptism. In Romans 6:3-5 the apostle Paul declares: "Or don't you know that all of us who were baptized into Christ Jesus were baptized into his death? We were therefore buried with him through baptism into death in order that, just as Christ was raised from the dead through the glory of the Father, we too may live a new life. If we have been united with him like this in his death, we will certainly also be united with him in his resurrection." Baptism is the likeness of His resurrection. It is a symbol that the believer has accepted the Lord of the resurrection as a personal life-giving Savior.

We have to keep in mind that the Bible says that the Sabbath is a memorial, not of the resurrection, but of Creation. Notice again in Exodus 20:11 the reason the fourth commandment gives for observing the Sabbath. "In six days the Lord made the heavens and the earth, the sea, and all that is in them, but he rested on the seventh day. Therefore the Lord blessed the Sabbath day and made it holy."

SABBATH IS THE SPECIAL TIME TO EXPLORE THE JOYS AND BEAUTY OF GOD'S CREATION.

PHOTODISC

The Sabbath is a weekly reminder that God is our Creator. Is it really just a coincidence that as human beings have lost sight of God's true Sabbath, many have also forgotten the truth of Creation?

God gave us the Sabbath not as a mere obligation, but as a gift. And this gift does even more than refresh our memories that God is our Father and Creator. As well as being a memorial of Creation, the Sabbath is a biblical symbol of sanctification. "Also I gave them my Sabbaths as a sign between us, so they would know that I the Lord made them holy," God told the prophet Ezekiel (Ezekiel 20:12). The King James Version uses the expression "I am the Lord that sanctify them."

"Sanctification" is one of those big theological words, but its meaning really isn't complicated or hard to understand. The word has to do with how God sets us apart for Himself, purifying us through His Spirit so as to prepare us to serve Him. And if you've ever tried to obey God on your own—to stop rebelling against Him—you know what a doomed effort that is without divine help. Sanctification means that in order to come to Jesus, we abandon our own efforts to clean up ourselves. Only He can transform us. And the Sabbath is a weekly symbol and reminder that God is our sanctifier.

A DAY OF REST

Finally, the Sabbath, as we've already noticed, is all about rest. And we're not talking here simply about physical rest—though it is included.

PHOTODISC

We live in a world in which the pace of life keeps accelerating dramatically. As people scramble to get ahead or just to pay the bills, they work long, stressful hours. But God never made us to labor like machines or to work seven days a week. And the God who created us knew that. So He made sure we would have one full day each week when we could set aside our work entirely and rest in every sense of the word. The best-selling *Catechism of the Catholic Church* correctly declares: "God's action is the model for human action. If God 'rested' . . . on the seventh day, man too ought to 'rest'" (2172).

But an even more important kind of rest the Sabbath brings to us is spiritual rest—resting from the hard work of trying in vain to obey God's laws through our own power, of trying to become more like Christ through our own efforts, of trying to overcome the sins and bad habits of our lives through our own strength.

The Sabbath reminds us that we can rest from our own attempts to make ourselves acceptable to God. For one thing, we are *already* accepted, even though we are still sinners! And for another, it's only through God's doing that any spiritual improvement can happen in our lives. Just as God created the world through His power, so He re-creates our hearts through that same mighty Creation power. The same God who brought the world into existence now makes a new heart in us. The Sabbath speaks to us of our incredible value in God's sight. We are special—God made us. Also we are unique. There is no one else like you or me in the universe. The Sabbath declares our specialness. It also speaks of our rest in Him—rest from our labors to save ourselves and of rest

THE SABBATH TEACHES US HOW TO ENJOY GOD'S GIFT OF LIFE.

in His grace, His ability to transform lives. The Sabbath is His day of grace, mercy, peace, rest, and power.

Some time ago Jill, a faithful Christian woman, was studying her Bible. "God," she said, "I don't want to know what humanity thinks. Just teach me from Your Word." Like Maria, the young Ukrainian girl whom we met at the beginning of this chapter, Jill was a truth seeker.

And as she studied, she weighed the issue of the Bible Sabbath. As she found in Scripture the various texts about the Sabbath, she wondered what day, indeed, is God's true worship day. In Revelation 1:10 she read, " 'On the Lord's Day I was in the Spirit.' " And she asked herself, "Is that Sunday? I need to find out." Matthew 12:8 told her that "the Son of Man is Lord of the Sabbath." Mark 2:28 stated that "the Son of Man is Lord even of the Sabbath." And Luke 6:5 also declared that "the Son of Man is Lord of the Sabbath." "There's only one conclusion," Jill said to herself. "The Sabbath is the true Lord's Day."

IF JESUS SAID THE SABBATH IS THE LORD'S DAY, I WANT TO FOLLOW HIM.

Wanting to follow Jesus, she began to search for a Sabbathkeeping church. If Jesus said the Sabbath is the Lord's Day, Jill told herself, "I want to follow Him."

Then she called her minister. "Pastor," she said, "I have a question. I want to find a church that observes the Bible Sabbath. I want to worship the Creator by honoring the same Sabbath that Adam kept, the same Sabbath taught in the Ten Commandments, the same Sabbath that Jesus, Paul, and John worshipped on. Pastor, what counsel do you have for me?"

Her pastor was a very wise person, and he said, "Jill, I don't know what others will advise you, but I counsel you to follow Jesus and God's law rather than human teachings. I counsel you, Jill, to walk right into the arms of Christ."

CHAPTER 9

STANDING GUARD

Many years ago, a story tells us, the czar of Russia was walking through a beautiful park near his palace. As he strolled along, he came upon a sentry guard—but the czar couldn't see anything the sentry should be protecting. "What is it that you're guarding?" he asked.

"Your Excellency," the man replied, "I'm not really sure. I'm just told to come here each day and do guard duty in this part of the park."

"Are you telling me," the czar responded, "that we're spending state money to have you guard something, and you don't even know what it is? I'll have to look into this."

So the czar searched the government archives. Soon he had his answer.

A hundred years earlier, he discovered, Catherine the Great had received a rosebush for her birthday. She had it planted and sent a soldier to the spot to guard it so no one would trample it and kill it. Each day someone transferred the order into the ledger for the next day so that a sentry would continue protecting the rosebush. And that tradition was passed down for more than 100 years.

But by this time the rosebush had long since died. So now the sentries were still standing guard in a remote part of the park—over nothing! They didn't even know what they were protecting. Someone stood guard over a nonexistent rosebush simply because it was a century-old tradition that no one—until the czar himself became curious—had bothered to question.

One time when Jesus was here on earth some religious leaders came to

Him complaining that His disciples had violated an old tradition they held sacred. Jesus began His answer by quoting Isaiah, an Old Testament prophet: "'These people honor me with their lips, but their hearts are far from me. They worship me in vain; their teachings are but rules taught by men.' You have let go of the commands of God and are holding on to the traditions of men" (Mark 7:6-8).

Do you think it's possible that today—just as in Christ's time—His church could be setting aside a commandment of God's to follow a human tradition instead? A tradition so old that almost no one knows how it started? A tradition nearly all Christians accept, thinking they are following God's law, when in fact they are following something of completely human origin?

"SAVAGE WOLVES WILL COME IN AMONG YOU AND WILL NOT SPARE THE FLOCK" (ACTS 20:29).

In the Old Testament the prophet Daniel wrote of a power that would rise up later and oppose God. It would, he said, "speak against the Most High and oppress his saints and try to change the set times and the laws" (Daniel 7:25). And Paul predicted that after the death of the apostles, Christ's church on earth would depart from true Bible faith. In Acts 20:28-30 he warned Christian leaders, "Keep watch over yourselves and all the flock. . . . After I leave," that is, after His death, "savage wolves will come in among you and will not spare the flock." As the church grew rapidly it was easy for false teachers to creep in from outside, bringing with them false philosophies and teachings.

But notice Acts 20:30: "Even from your own number men will arise and distort the truth in order to draw away disciples after them." Paul was in effect saying, "Beware even of leaders in the church! Just because they may have been in the church a long time, that doesn't mean they cannot slip into error. Leaders will rise up and wander from scriptural teaching a little bit here and a little bit there. Beware of that." The church faced danger not only from outside. Even those who might have grown up in it could also lead it astray. The apostle was appealing to the early Christians to stay by the Bible and by what Jesus had taught.

Notice also Paul's concern in 2 Thessalonians 2:7: "The secret power of lawlessness is already at work." Already, he was saying, he saw a deadly trend in the church—a trend of drifting away from Scripture and God's law. Satan was using forces within the church to destroy it.

Looking back now on history, we're able to see how God's law became compromised. The prophecies of Daniel and Revelation both reveal God's plans and unmask the wiles of the adversary in the last days. You may be wondering who led the church to abandon the Sabbath and adopt the first day of the week for worship. How did the Christian worship day get changed? Why did it happen? And when and by whom?

In order to answer these vital questions, I want to take you on a journey into the prophecies of the book of Daniel. In an earlier chapter we learned in Daniel 2 how God unlocked a puzzling dream that Nebuchadnezzar, the king of Babylon, had. Now in Daniel 7 we will see how one night the prophet himself had a dream. And in that dream he saw animals rise up out of the sea. His dream not only deals with events in his day—the time of Babylon—but also takes us through the reigns of Medo-Persia, Greece, and Rome. Even beyond that, it guides us through Christianity's early days and shows how, after the time of Christ and His disciples, a *power that would attempt to transfer the Sabbath would arise*.

DANIEL'S AMAZING DREAM

The prophet woke up troubled, thinking about what he had dreamed. He recognized that his dream had great importance and significance. "In the first year of Belshazzar, king of Babylon, Daniel had a dream, and visions passed through his mind as he was lying on his bed. He wrote down the substance of his dream" (Daniel 7:1). In his dream he saw four great beasts rise up out of the sea. The first seemed to be a lion and had eagle's wings. A second beast resembled a bear elevated on one side, with three ribs in its mouth. The third was like a leopard with four heads and with four wings on its back.

Harry Baerg

"After that," Daniel continued, "in my vision at night I looked, and there before me was a fourth beast—terrifying and frightening and very powerful. It had large iron teeth; it crushed and devoured its victims and trampled underfoot whatever was left. It was different from all the former beasts, and it had ten horns" (verse 7).

The previous beasts had been strange enough, but the fourth one was indescribable—not like a lion, a leopard, a bear, or *anything* that Daniel had ever seen before! It was a dreadful, powerful creature with iron teeth, bronze claws (verse 19), and 10 horns.

Daniel's dream foretold the struggle between good and evil.

Next, among those 10 horns, the prophet watched another horn come up. In biblical symbolism horns represent power and those agencies that use it. This horn was little at first, but as the prophet watched, it became a great power: "This horn had eyes like the eyes of a man and a mouth that spoke boastfully" (verse 8). And this little horn, we shall soon learn, tried to change the law of God! It said that divine law *could* and *should* be changed. What could this prophecy mean?

"Oh," some might argue, "prophecy is just guesswork. We can only speculate about who the lion and the bear are, as well as what the other beasts emerging from the sea and the sea itself represent." But wait a moment. *Who* gave Daniel the dream? God did. And if He sent the dream, wouldn't you think He would also provide us some way to interpret it? Do you think that when it comes to understanding prophecy, it's every person for themselves? Peter reminds us: "No prophecy of the scripture is of any private interpretation" (2 Peter 1:20, KJV). That means I shouldn't

EMPIRES REVEALED

DANIEL 2 THE GREAT IMAGE	EMPIRE	DANIEL 7 THE FOUR BEASTS
head of gold	**BABYLON** (605—539 B.C.)	lion with eagle's wings
breast and arms of silver	**MEDIA-PERSIA** (539—331 B.C.)	bear with three ribs
thighs of brass	**GREECE** (331—168 B.C.)	leopard with wings and four heads
legs of iron	**ROME** (168 B.C. — middle of fourth century)	dragonlike beast with 10 horns
feet of iron and clay	**DIVIDED EMPIRE** (A.D. 351—A.D. 476.)	10 horns
	1260 YEARS (A.D. 538—A.D.1798) papal supremacy	time, times and a half time little horn
	1844—END-TIME	judgment
rock smites image	**SOON**	Christ's kingdom

have to depend on what I personally think the prophecy means.

THE BIBLE EXPLAINS ITSELF

The Word of God consistently explains itself. Let's go to Scripture and discover the meaning of each of the symbols. Daniel wrote that the little-horn power would "speak against the Most High and oppress his saints and *try to change the set times and the laws*" (Daniel 7:25). The prophecy must pertain to *divine* laws, since throughout history rulers and governments have continually altered human ones. So we can be sure, first of all, that the little-horn power intends to "change the times and the law" (verse 25, RSV) in God's realm, not the human sphere.

The core of God's law is the Ten Commandments. The only commandment that involves *time* is the *fourth* commandment regarding the *Sabbath*. But note that the prophecy said that the little horn would try to change the law. Can any earthly agency *really* alter that law written with God's own finger? No! No human being can, but the little horn would dare to attempt to do exactly that!

Let's take a careful look at the prophecy. What do the lion, the bear, the leopard, and the various other symbols represent? And did the little horn actually try to tamper with divine law?

To answer those questions, we must let Scripture itself explain the meaning of his dream. "Four great beasts . . . came up out of the sea" (verse 3). Thus the first symbol we will deal with is the sea. What does it stand for? Bible scholars have recognized for a long time that we should study the prophetic books of Daniel and Revelation together. So let's read Revelation 17:15: "The *waters* you saw . . . are peoples, multitudes, nations and languages." So waters can represent people—many people.

Please don't misunderstand. When you read "water" in the Bible, it usually stands for literal, physical water. But when Jesus says, "Drink the water of life," He's speaking figuratively. When a word is obviously literal, Bible students should stick to the literal meaning unless they encounter a compelling reason for adopting a figurative or symbolic sense. But in the *prophecies* of Daniel and Revelation, which talk about beasts coming out of the sea—a lion with eagle's wings or a leopard with four heads or an indescribable beast with 10 horns—we can be sure we're reading a passage with all kinds of *symbols*.

THE BIBLE OFTEN USES WATER AS A SYMBOL OF NATIONS AND PEOPLES.

PHOTODISC

So we look for a symbolic sense. Revelation 17:15 thus tells us clearly that in symbol-loaded prophecy "the waters" (or "the sea") represent people.

What about the winds? Daniel says that in his dream "the four winds of heaven [were] churning up the great sea. Four great beasts . . . came up out of the sea" (Daniel 7:2, 3). What do winds stand for when used as a prophetic Bible symbol? Just as literal winds, such as a hurricane or a tornado, cause physical destruction, so "winds" in prophecy depict political or social strife and turmoil—as we say today when we talk about "the winds of war."

"WINDS" IN PROPHECY DEPICT POLITICAL OR SOCIAL STRIFE AND TURMOIL.

For instance, God pronounced the doom of the enemy nation of Elam in Jeremiah 49:36, 37: "I will bring against Elam the four *winds* from the four quarters of the heaven; I will scatter them to the four winds, and there will not be a nation where Elam's exiles do not go. . . . I will pursue them with the sword." In Daniel 11:40 the prophet uses the same metaphor of winds to represent war: "The king of the north shall come against him *like a whirlwind,* with chariots, and with horsemen, and with many ships" (KJV).

UNLOCKING THE SYMBOLS

So far, we've established that the sea represents peoples and the winds war. Symbolic prophecy—God's "sign language"—is easily understood if we let the Bible act as its own interpreter. Next, God tells us plainly in Daniel 7:17-23 that "the four great *beasts* are four kingdoms that will rise. . . . The fourth beast is a fourth *kingdom.*" So these beasts are not just four individual kings, but rather four successive kingdoms or empires. Therefore, when the Bible talks about beasts coming up out of a windy sea, it's depicting the rise of kingdoms through the turmoil of war. We have let the Bible explain itself.

PHOTODISC

Even today we use animals as symbols. People in the United States regard an elephant as a symbol of the Republican Party and a donkey of the Democrats. Americans use the eagle as a symbol of the United States. England's symbol has traditionally been a lion. For many years people recognized the Russian bear as a symbol of that country. Just as we still use animals as symbols to stand for nations today, so God employs them too. But which kingdoms or nations do the beasts in Daniel's dream specifically represent?

As if to underline the great lessons presented in Daniel 2, God gives a kind of instant replay in Daniel 7. Chapters 2 and 7 of Daniel's wonderful book contain some remarkable parallels. Both chapters are clearly prophetic rather than historical in nature. Each chapter features a God-given dream filled with vital information. You'll recall from an earlier chapter that God inspired the prophet Daniel to interpret King Nebuchadnezzar's dream of a great image. Daniel 2 focused on four symbolic metals—gold, silver, bronze, and iron. Now Daniel 7 employs four symbolic animals—a lion, a bear, a leopard, and a monstrous beast.

THE VISIONS OF DANIEL 2 AND DANIEL 7 PARALLEL EACH OTHER.

The image of Daniel 2, with its head of gold, breast and arms of silver, belly and thighs of bronze, legs of iron, and feet of iron and clay, represents the four kingdoms that would rule the world of the Bible: Babylon, Medo-Persia, Greece, and Rome. The four beasts of Daniel 7, as we shall see, also symbolize the same four empires.

In Daniel 2 the prophet declared that the image's head of gold stood for Babylon. Now in Daniel 7 the first beast was a lion with eagle's wings that *also* represented Babylon. As you will remember, the Babylonian Empire ruled from 605 to 539 B.C. Interestingly, archaeologists have uncovered in the ruins of Babylon the symbol of the lion with eagle's wings on tiled walls, such as those along the "Procession Street" leading to the main temple enclosure of the city. The eagle's wings on the lion denote

BABYLON

the empire's ability to conquer rapidly. Speaking of the Chaldeans or Babylonians, Habakkuk 1:8 says that their horses were "swifter than the leopards. . . . They shall *fly as the eagle* that hasteth to eat" (KJV). Jeremiah 4:7 and 13 speak of Babylon, God's instrument to punish Israel for its sins, as a "lion" and says that "his chariots come like a whirlwind, his horses are *swifter than eagles*." The lion with eagle's wings was an appropriate symbol for Babylon.

But Babylon fell to the Medes and Persians. In Daniel 2 the second metal, silver, represented Medo-Persia. Daniel 7 speaks of a second beast, a bear humped up on one side with three ribs in its mouth. The Medes and Persians formed a dual kingdom, but the Persians were decidedly the more powerful of the two factions. So the Persians raised themselves up over the Medes.

Furthermore, the Bible says the bear "had three ribs in its mouth" (Daniel 7:5). Medo-Persia ruled the world from 539 to 331 B.C., but in order to gain world dominion it had to conquer three great nations. First it attacked Babylon. Next it moved north to seize Lydia, the land of the fabulously wealthy King Croesus, located in the modern country of Turkey. Then it invaded Egypt. The Medo-Persians were ferocious like a bear, and the three ribs in its mouth represented its three great conquests of Babylon, Lydia, and Egypt—three major nations, exactly as the Bible predicted.

MEDO-PERSIA

A third metal, bronze, in Daniel 2 symbolized a third world power, Greece. The Greek Empire ruled from 331 to 168 B.C. In Daniel 7 the third animal was a leopard—but with four wings and four heads. If wings upon the Babylonian lion signified rapidity of conquest, we can conclude that they imply the same here. The leopard is naturally a swift beast, so if you want to depict speed, you might choose a leopard. But if you desired to indicate exceptional speed, you could put wings on the animal. Even the two wings the lion had were not sufficient here—the leopard had four, denoting the incredibly fast conquests of the Greek leader Alexander the Great, who conquered much of the then-known world by the time he was 33.

PROPHECY PRECISELY FULFILLED

How many heads does the leopard have? Four. Why four? Because Alexander died without appointing an heir to his throne, and after about a dozen years of turmoil his four generals divided the empire among themselves. Their names were Cassander, Lysimachus, Ptolemy, and Seleucus.

How did the Bible know that Alexander would conquer so quickly or that his empire would eventually split among four successors? Bible prophecy is history told in advance and carries its own credentials of divine accuracy.

Finally, Daniel 2 tells of the fourth metal, iron, comprising the legs of the image that represent the Roman Empire. So very fittingly Daniel 7 describes "a fourth beast—terrifying and frightening and very powerful. It had large *iron* teeth. . . . And it had ten horns" (Daniel 7:7). As we learned before, Rome ruled the world from 168 B.C. to A.D. 476. But Rome wouldn't be conquered by a fifth major human power. The 10 horns indicate that the Roman Empire would be divided and remain that way.

At this point in Daniel 2 we've reached the feet of the image, and the dream jumps ahead to the rock that smites the image, symbolizing, as we shall see, the coming of Jesus and the end of the world. But Daniel 7, with its 10 horns, gives us more information. God covers the same ground in both chapters, but here in Daniel 7 He adds further details because He wants to get past the breakup of the Roman Empire. As we learn what happened next, we will discover who attempted to replace the Sabbath.

Daniel 7:24 tells us that "the ten horns are ten kings who will come from this kingdom." So Rome would fall, fragmenting into smaller kingdoms. And history records exactly that. Bible prophecy is accurate. Barbarian tribes—such as the Huns—invaded and carved up the once-great Roman Empire. The various tribes settled in different places. For example, the Franks took over the area we know as France. As the empire fell apart, the Visigoths occupied what is now Spain; the Suevi, Portugal; the Lombards, Italy; and so forth. Europe, North Africa, Palestine, and other parts of the former Roman Empire became a mosaic of smaller nations.

The prophetic story has now progressed to the early centuries of the church, after the death of Christ and His disciples. As the empire began to totter, something astonishing would happen in Rome: "I considered the [10] horns, and behold, there came up among them another horn, a little one, before which three of the first horns were plucked up by the roots; and behold, in this horn were eyes like the eyes of a man, and a mouth speaking great things" (verse 8, RSV).

THE MYSTERIOUS LITTLE HORN

What was God trying to tell us when He sent the prophecy about this little-horn power? As we have already mentioned, in the Bible a horn represents a kingdom or power—religious or political. Daniel says that a little horn would become prominent in the days of those 10 horns. It would be a minor power at first, but in time it would grow "exceeding great" (Daniel 8:9, KJV).

The prophet saw some differences between the little horn and the 10 horns already noted. The first thing Daniel observed different about it was that it emerged *after* Rome had fragmented into smaller kingdoms. Daniel 7:24 says that "the ten horns are ten kings who will come from this kingdom [of Rome]. After them another king [the little horn] will arise." The little-horn power thus chronologically became prominent after the establishment of the 10 kingdoms—that is, after Rome's collapse and subsequent breakup.

ROME

The passage also indicates the location of the little-horn power. We can say with certainty that geographically it had to develop within the territory of the old Roman Empire. Daniel 7:8 comments that as Daniel considered the 10 horns of the divided Roman Empire, "a little horn" sprouted up "among them." It would not emerge in South America, eastern Asia, or anywhere else that had not been part of Roman territory.

Daniel 7:7 specifically declares that the little-horn power would be "different from" the previous 10. The first 10 horns developed from divisions of the Roman Empire, regions that became the basis for the modern nations of the Mediterranean world. They were and are all *political* in nature. But the little-horn power would be different in that it proved to be a religious power (or at least a hybrid, being part *religious* and part *political*—a religiopolitical entity).

Daniel 7:8 emphasizes that the little horn had "a mouth that spoke boastfully." Furthermore, Daniel 7:11 indicates that "the boastful words the horn was speaking" fascinated the prophet. Finally, Daniel 7:25 says that the little-horn power "will speak *against the Most High*." Clearly, then, God is telling us that this religious power, which was both different from all the political powers of the former Roman Empire and which would emerge in Rome after the breakup of the Roman Empire, would make great claims and issue great decrees. Boastfully, it would even claim authority to change divine law, including the day of worship!

Sadly Daniel testifies that as he watched, "this horn was waging war against the saints and defeating them" (verse 21). The Bible here foretells religious persecution, for "the saints" are God's faithful people. The little horn used force against those who disagreed with it. The Middle Ages especially saw many faithful Christians suffer and even die for what they believed was the true faith, some languishing in dungeons, others burned at the stake. Daniel 7:25 predicted that the little horn would "oppress [God's] saints," and history has tragically verified that it happened.

GOD WANTS YOU TO KNOW

Evidently God thinks it's important for us to understand these things, because He gives many clues to help us identify this mysterious power. Let's review briefly those we have covered so far:

1. This power would arise *after* the breakup of the Roman Empire. This point is important, because it means that the attempted change of the Sabbath and God's law would occur after Christ's death.
2. The little horn arises *among* the first 10 horns—that is to say, out of the divisions of the Roman Empire.
3. It had *eyes* like those of a man—apparently the symbol of human intelligence.
4. The little horn would be *different* from the first 10 horns. The first horns were all *political* powers, but this power would be a religious entity.
5. The little-horn power had not only "eyes like the eyes of a man" but also a *mouth* that spoke "boastfully" (verse 20)—even "*great words against the most High*" (verse 25, KJV).
6. At times the little horn would use its power to persecute God's people. It "*was waging war*" (verse 21) with them and would "*wear out*" (verse 25, KJV) the saints of the Most High, prevailing against them.

When you line up all the identifying features of the little-horn power, its identity becomes remarkably clear. The Bible says the attempted change of God's law would come *not* from the disciples in Jerusalem, but from the early church itself.

By the time of Emperor Constantine in the early A.D. 300s the great Roman Empire had begun to crumble. The Jews had revolted against the Romans several times during the first and second centuries. The Bar Kochba uprising during the early A.D. 130s nearly caused the financial collapse of the empire because of the horrendous cost of putting down the rebellion. The various revolts caused the Jews to be unpopular. Since the early Christians, like the Jews, continued to observe the seventh day—Saturday—as the Sabbath, many Romans mistook them as yet another Jewish sect and persecuted them just as they did the Jews.

Constantine established the first Sunday law in A.D. 321.

Christians, of course, weren't happy being mistaken for Jews because of the Sabbath. They wanted clear distinctions between them and the Jews. Also Christians felt frustrated by their lack of success in communicating Christianity to a pagan culture. The pagans felt much more comfortable with the worship of the gods of their ancestors, including the sun god. To be a true Roman was to worship Roman gods. Many Christian apologists sought to find common ground between Christianity and Roman culture as they attempted to defend Christian teaching. Sometimes they adopted philosophies and customs that actually undermined Christian teachings.

Early in the fourth century Constantine began to accept Christianity. Desperate to unite his tottering empire, Constantine adopted a number of measures that he felt would bring many of its clashing elements together. One of them involved Sunday. After all, Christ had risen from the dead on Sunday. Christians apparently had a long tradition of holding brief worship services Sunday morning before going off to work (Didache 7.381; Justin Martyr 1.186). As for the pagans, they worshipped the sun god. If Christians united with the pagans in worshipping on Sunday, they would further disassociate themselves from the unpopular Jews and further establish points of contact between them and the majority of the Roman population.

By this time in the early history of the Christian church the single most powerful leader of the church in the Roman Empire had become the bishop of Rome. The Roman emperor encouraged the developing power of the leadership in Rome. Constantine felt that one strong church would help hold the empire together. So the state powers worked together with church leaders to make changes that they thought would strengthen the empire.

TRANSFERRING SABBATH TO SUNDAY

Church leaders took the solemnity of the seventh-day Sabbath and sought to transfer it to Sunday, piously declaring that they had the authority to change even divine laws, because, after all, they were the church leaders.

And for his part, Emperor Constantine imposed the first Sunday law. In A.D. 321 he proclaimed: "On the venerable Day of the Sun, let the magistrates and people residing in cities rest, and let all the workshops be closed." Constantine's civil legislation was soon incorporated into church teaching and practice—first by the Council of Laodicea in A.D. 364, and later by other ecclesiastical councils, church synods, and papal pronouncements.

The Council of Laodicea declared that "Christians must not judaize by resting on the Sabbath but must work on that day, rather honoring the Lord's Day; if they can, resting then as Christians. But if any shall be found to be judaizers, let them be anathema for Christ."

You must not rest but work on Saturday, the church said. And you must honor Sunday and, if possible, not work that day. If you are found "judaizing"—that is, being like the Jews and observing the Sabbath—you are to be anathema, cut off from Christ.

Perhaps some readers may be thinking, *This is just a wild idea. Where do you find this documented by the church?* The church itself acknowledges that it happened!

Here is a very clear statement from a catechism, a collection of questions and answers used to instruct prospective church members. This one is *The Convert's Catechism of Catholic Doctrine,* long used for all who joined the Catholic Church. Notice what it says:

"**Q.** *Which is the Sabbath day?"*

"**A.** Saturday is the Sabbath day."

Notice how it continues:

"**Q.** *Why do we observe Sunday instead of Saturday?"*

"**A.** We observe Sunday instead of Saturday because the Catholic Church transferred the solemnity from Saturday to Sunday" (1957 ed., p. 50).

On page 174 of A *Doctrinal Catechism*, Stephen Keenan asks the question: "*Have you any other way of proving that the Church has power to institute festivals of precept?*" He then answers: "Had she not such power, she could not have done that in which all modern religionists agree with her—she could not have substituted the observance of Sunday, the first day of the week, for the observance of Saturday, the seventh day, a change for which there is no Scriptural authority" (third American edition).

Notice now a comment from a book written by James Cardinal Gibbons. Cardinal Gibbons was a brilliant scholar and one of the leading lights of American Catholicism. He wrote a book called *The Faith of Our Fathers*, which sold millions of copies. On page 89 he stated: "You may read the Bible from Genesis to Revelation, and you will not find a single line authorizing the sanctification of Sunday. The Scriptures enforce the religious observance of Saturday."

The question is this: Did the church have the authority to alter God's law?

In Malachi 3:6 God said, "I . . . do not change." We have an unchangeable God who says, as we find it in Matthew 5:17 and 18: "Do not think that I have come to abolish the Law or the Prophets; I have not come to abolish them but to fulfill them. I tell you the truth, until heaven and earth disappear, not the smallest letter, not the least stroke of a pen, will by any means disappear from the Law until everything is accomplished."

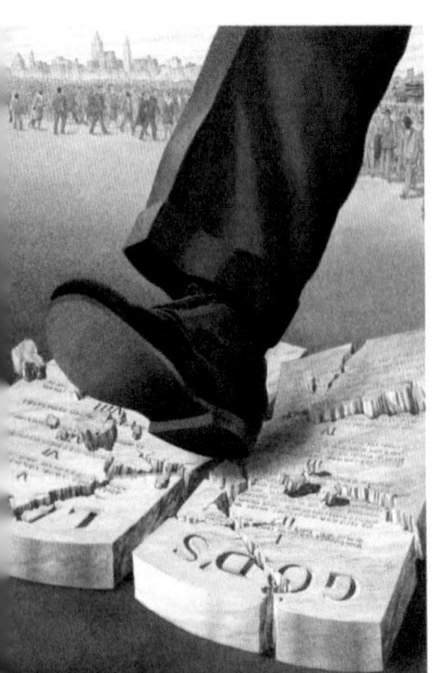

On the other hand, Daniel predicted that the church would attempt to change the law. The Bible told us it would happen! Do you see why God is calling us back to worshipping the Creator today through His final warning message to the world in Revelation 14:7: "Worship him who made the heavens, the earth, the sea and the springs of water"—that is, worship your Creator? As the 1994 *Catechism of the Catholic Church* correctly acknowledges, "in speaking of the sabbath Scripture recalls creation" (2169). And do you understand why Revelation 14:12 declares of God's last-day people that they "obey God's commandments"?

People sometimes wonder *What difference does a day make?* The fact is that if it were simply a matter of days, it would not matter much at all. But the issue is much more than a day. It revolves around God's commandments—His law. The Sabbath is thus far more than a matter of one day versus another. It is an issue of allegiance and loyalty. The real question is Will we be obedient to God—or will we follow human tradition? Will we do what God says, or will we accept what religious leaders teach contrary to the Word of God? In the final analysis, either we will decide to obey God's commandments, or we will accept a change of that same law made by misguided religious leaders.

The evidence that human beings have attempted to change the Sabbath is clear. Each of us must decide how we will respond to it. There are just two sides in the great conflict between good and evil, between love and selfishness, between Christ and Satan. And God has chosen to test our allegiance and loyalty to Him through the Sabbath commandment. Will we obey Him and keep the seventh day holy? Or will we worship instead on a day based on human tradition?

It's time to choose who has your allegiance and loyalty.

NEW TESTAMENT PASSAGES REVEALING THE IMPORTANCE OF GOD'S LAW

Matthew 5:17-19; 15:3-6; 19:17; Mark 7:8, 9; 10:19; 12:28, 29; Luke 1:6; 15:29; 18:20; 23:56; John 10:18; 12:49, 50; 14:15, 21; 15:10-12; Romans 2:7-13; 1 Corinthians 7:19; 1 Timothy 6:14; 2 Peter 2:21; 3:2; Ephesians 6:2; 1 John 2:3, 4, 7, 8; 3:22-24; 4:21; 5:3, 4; 2 John 4-6; Revelation 14:12; 12:17; 22:14.

CHAPTER 10

HOW CAN WE AVOID THE MARK OF THE BEAST?

You bring your shopping cart to the checkout counter and unload its contents onto the conveyer belt. But at stores nationwide this is the first day of a major change in the checkout process. Instead of scanning just your items, the store also scans you. And you see a message flash onto the electronic register. "Customer declined," it announces.

Suddenly security officers surround you and take you aside to question you at length. They demand to know why you don't have the required biochip implant that contains all your personal information—including your permission to buy or sell. Further, they quiz you as to why you don't have the tattoo high on your forehead near the hairline. You don't have the mark—the loyalty mark of the beast. And now your life is in danger.

Could a scene such as this ever become a future reality? Many best-selling books today say yes. But is this really what the Bible says about the mark of the beast? Or is what we've just described complete fiction? In this chapter we'll explore what Scripture has to say about these vital questions.

During the past few years the phenomenal success of two series has astounded the publishing world: the Harry Potter series, by British author J. K. Rowling, and the Left Behind series, by Christian authors Tim LaHaye and Jerry Jenkins. At the moment I want to focus on the Left Behind books.

This 12-book series (with three more promised), released between 1995 and 2004, has sold well in excess of 75 million copies, making its authors and its publisher, Tyndale House, extremely wealthy. It is a fic-

WHO IS THE BEAST?

The beast represents a religious-political system that attempts to usurp the authority of God by changing His law, enforcing an economic boycott against those who oppose it, and eventually imposing a death decree upon all those who do not yield to its commands.

tional, yet supposedly Bible-based, preview of the end-times of Planet Earth. The books teach a secret rapture, a seven-year tribulation prior to the second coming of Jesus Christ, and the rise of an evil world dictator called the antichrist—the "beast" power of the Bible books of Daniel and Revelation. This villainous leader, the books say, will use a loyalty mark to enforce his will on the world's people.

The eighth book in the series has as its title *The Mark: The Beast Rules the World.* In this book the antichrist—a powerful individual named Nicolae Carpathia—has miraculously risen from the dead. He has his followers branded with a tattooed loyalty mark in their hand or forehead—and "vaccinated" with a biochip containing all their personal information. Those who refuse the mark lose the right to buy or sell anything. Should they continue to reject it, they face execution.

But let's pause and consider another best-selling book. It has sold far more copies than all of the Left Behind and Harry Potter books combined. Not only does it discuss the antichrist; it describes the beast, its mark, and the mysterious number 666. And it too predicts a time when no one without the mark can buy or sell.

But the story it tells is worlds apart from the fiction of the Left Behind series. The Bible—God's own reliable Word to you and me—contains only truth, not speculation. Millions of people read books about prophecy without ever examining what the Bible prophets themselves actually say.

When people study the book of Revelation, they often ask, "What is this beast power? And what is the mark of the beast? Is the beast a supercomputer, as some claim? an organization? a person?"

And others, especially the fans of the Left Behind fiction series, wonder if the mark of the beast might indeed be an implanted biochip—just as the authors present it. Others speculate that perhaps the mark could be a bar code—like the row of bars printed on products for sale and scanned in many countries at checkout counters.

According to the Bible, the real mark of the beast is far more than a computer chip or bar code. God's Word tells us exactly what it is—and how to avoid receiving it.

Revelation 14:9 and 10 issues a terrifying warning: "If anyone worships the beast and his image and receives his mark on the forehead or on the hand, he, too, will drink of the wine of God's fury, which has been poured full strength into the cup of his wrath."

If getting this mark has such dire consequences, what exactly is it, and how can we avoid receiving it?

In Revelation 13:1 the apostle John described how he "saw a beast coming out of the sea. He had ten horns and seven heads, with ten crowns on his horns, and on each head a blasphemous name." As we observed previously, the prophecy weaves together several Bible symbols. An animal in Bible prophecy, as explained in Daniel 7:23, represents an earthly power or kingdom. Water, as revealed in Revelation 17:15, denotes people.

The beast in Revelation 13, then, is a power or kingdom, emerging from among a multitude of people. The prophetic symbol has seven heads and 10 crowns. It is a composite beast. John employs the very same animal symbols as those used by Daniel in describing the great powers in Daniel 7. You will remember that Daniel's book made clear that the lion represented Babylon; the bear, Medo-Persia; the leopard, Greece; and the ferocious and indescribable beast, the Roman Empire.

A BEAST WITH SEVEN CHARACTERISTICS

The beast of Revelation 13 succeeds these four great empires, and as John saw it in vision, it consisted of parts of each of Daniel's symbols. Scripture describes it as having seven characteristics. Only one entity on earth has all the traits found in this prophecy. Both Scripture and secular history make its identification certain. We don't need to rely on human-made fiction to tell us what the Bible makes so clear.

Revelation 13:2 provides the first clue to the beast's identity. Speaking of it, John wrote: "The dragon gave the beast his power and his throne and great authority." Did the dragon power—which the Bible prophecies of Daniel and Revelation make plain is a symbol of Satan working through the pagan Roman Empire—ever give its power and authority to any succeeding entity? The answer is yes! And what received that power and authority? On May 11, 330, Constantine, the emperor of Rome, decided to move the seat of his empire from Rome to Byzantium. He named the new capital Noma Roma, but it became known as Constantinople.

Constantine certainly didn't want to leave Rome in a political vacuum, but he also didn't want to turn it over to a national political leader who might become a future threat to his own power. So instead he offered control of the city, along with a treasury and an army, to its religious leader, the bishop of Rome.

During early Christian history church and state increasingly interfered in each other's affairs.

Historian Thomas Stanley describes the shift from a political power to a religious hierarchy in these words

Siegfried Horn Mlseum/Nathan Greene

THE BEAST IS NOT

a computer in Belgium

a powerful earthly political leader

a child born in the Middle East

a single religious leader

a Roman emperor

THE BEAST IS

a religious-political system

on page 40 of his book *The History of Philosophy:* "The popes filled the place of the vacant emperors of Rome, inheriting their power, prestige, and titles from paganism. . . . Constantine left all to the Bishop of Rome. . . . The papacy is but the ghost of the deceased Roman Empire, sitting crowned upon its grave." Professor Lablanca, professor of history at the University of Rome, forcefully states, "To the succession of the Caesars came the succession of the Pontiffs in Rome."

Pagan Rome's authority became that of papal Rome. So here is the first clue to the identity of the beast. Is it possible that papal Rome also fits the other identifying characteristics given in Revelation?

Let's notice John's second clue: The beast power of Revelation 13 would be primarily religious and demand worship. Verse 4 makes this point plain: "Men worshiped the dragon because he had given authority to the beast, and they also worshiped the beast and asked, 'Who is like the beast? Who can make war against him?' "

This second characteristic emphasizes how different this beast power is compared to earlier empires. Its influence would extend far beyond its own geographical boundaries, not primarily in the realm of politics, but in the arena of religion.

The entity envisioned in Revelation 13 is far more than political in nature. It is a worldwide religious power demanding worship. Many mistake this entity as a person. In the Bible the symbol of beast or animal represents a system or organization either political or religious. Other commentators depict the beast as an atheistic unbeliever. But the Bible describes something totally different. The "beast" represents a system of religion that has departed from the fundamental principles of Scripture. It establishes the authority of priests and prelates, church councils and decrees, and tradition and dogma above the Word of God.

The third characteristic of the beast John points to is in verse 5: "The

WHAT IS THE MARK OF THE BEAST?

The mark of the beast is the exaltation of human religious tradition in the place of God's commandments. It places humanity's way above the divine, and church dogma above inspired revelation. A counterfeit system of worship will ultimately attempt to substitute itself for the Creator's Sabbath.

beast was given a mouth to utter proud words and blasphemies." Blasphemy is a Bible term—not one used by civil governments. It applies to anyone or anything that impersonates God, assumes His titles of office or His authority, or presumes to exercise the special privileges belonging to Him alone. Does the Papacy claim any of these divine powers or privileges?

Pope Leo XIII, in an encyclical letter dated June 30, 1894, declared: "We hold upon this earth the place of God Almighty" (cited in *The Great Encyclical Letters of Pope Leo XIII*, p. 304).

The Pharisees criticized Jesus for claiming to forgive sins (Mark 2:3-7; cf. Isaiah 43:25). They correctly realized that only God could do that—and Jesus was God. But it is not something that human beings can do. Yet consider the following claim in *The Catholic Priest*: "Seek where you will, through heaven and earth, and you will find but one created being who can forgive the sinner. . . . That extraordinary being is the priest, the [Roman] Catholic priest" (pp. 78, 79).

And from *Dignity and Duties of the Priest*, a handbook for priests by Alphonsus de Liguori, we read: "God himself is obliged to abide by the judgment of his priests, and either not to pardon or to pardon, according as they refuse or give absolution. . . . The sentence of the priest precedes, and God subscribes to it" (p. 27).

The church claims that its priests have the privilege and prerogatives of God to forgive sins. Yet the Bible is clear that there is only "one mediator between God and men, the man Christ Jesus, who gave himself as a ransom for all" (1 Timothy 2:5).

Revelation 13:7 provides the next identifying trait of the beast power: "He was given power to make war against the saints and to conquer them."

Has the church ever persecuted dissenters? Conservative estimates place the number of Christians martyred by the state church during the

Dark Ages in the millions. Whole communities perished for no other crime than that of "heresy"—daring to believe or teach something contrary to established doctrine or practice. Note this from the church publication called *Western Watchman of St. Louis*, December 24, 1908: "The church has persecuted. Only a tyro [one uninformed] in church history will deny that." Or consider another amazing statement from the book *Institutes of Public Ecclesiastical Law*, written by P. Marianus de Luca: "The Church may, by divine right, confiscate the property of heretics, imprison their persons and condemn them to the flames. . . . In this age, the right to inflict the severest penalties, even death, belongs to the Church. . . . There is no graver offense than heresy. . . . It must be rooted out" (vol. 2, p. 142).

The next characteristic of the beast power requires that we examine some biblical mathematics. Revelation 13:5 revealed that the beast received the power to continue "for forty-two months." A careful study of prophetic chronology in the Bible reveals that Scripture uses the symbol of a prophetic month of 30 days. As we have seen previously, Ezekiel 4:6 indicates that a day stands for a year in Bible prophecy. The book of Revelation states that the beast's power would last for 42 times 30 prophetic days, equaling 1,260 prophetic days, or 1,260 actual years.

At first pagans persecuted Christians. As time went on, Christians began to persecute each other.

History tells us that by A.D. 538 the papal government had conquered the last of the three major powers in conflict with it. The bishop of Rome had secured his religiopolitical throne, marking the beginning of papal supremacy. Adding 1,260 years to A.D. 538, we arrive at A.D. 1798.

At this point, as described by

John in Revelation 13:3, one of the heads of the beast "seemed to have had a fatal wound." Did something happen to wound the papal power in 1798? Indeed it did!

In that year the emperor Napoleon Bonaparte sent the French general Louis Alexandre Berthier to Rome to take the pope captive. Notice the historical account of this event as it appears on page 24 of the book *Church History*: "The murder of a Frenchman in Rome in 1798 gave the French an excuse for occupying the Eternal City and putting an end to the Papal temporal power. The aged Pontiff himself was carried off into exile to Valence. . . . The enemies of the Church rejoiced. The last Pope, they declared, had reigned" (see also Richard Duppa, *A Brief Account of the Subversion of the Papal Government*, 2nd ed., pp. 46, 47).

Had Napoleon and "the enemies of the church" consulted Scripture, they would have realized that the papal system was not finished, only wounded. Revelation 13:3 says: "The fatal wound had been healed. The whole world was astonished and followed the beast."

One day the deadly wound inflicted in 1798 would heal, opening the way for the Papacy to regain its universal influence and set the stage for a dramatic role in the last days.

The sixth identifying characteristic of the beast appears in Revelation 13:18: "This calls for wisdom. If anyone has insight, let him calculate the number of the beast, for it is man's number. His number is 666."

After revealing these six identifying characteristics of the beast, the prophet John foretells how the beast will use its power to force all humanity to comply with the beast's demands in the last days. It brings us to the mysterious mark of the beast described in Revelation 13:16 and 17: "He also forced everyone, small and great, rich and poor, free and slave, to receive a mark on his right hand or on his forehead, so that no one could buy or sell unless he had the mark, which is the name of the beast or the number of his name."

This mark has been the focus of many interpretations. Some interpret it literally, relating it to everything from bar codes on store packaging to high-powered computer chips imprinted on driver's licenses or even implanted under the skin. But according to the Bible's description of those who do not receive the beast's mark, the "mark" is not a physical thing, but actually a symbol of rebellion or disloyalty to God's government. Revelation 14:12 says that those who do not receive it "obey God's commandments and remain faithful to Jesus."

Revelation 13 and 14 make clear that one group of people will receive the mark of the beast. The other will also receive a mark—but it will not come from the beast! Notice Revelation 7:2 and 3: "Then I saw another angel coming up from the east, having the seal of the living God. He called out in a loud voice to the four angels who had been given power to harm the land and the sea: 'Do not harm the land or the sea or the trees until we put a seal on the foreheads of the servants of our God.' "

THE MARK OF THE BEAST IS NOT A COMPUTER CHIP OR ANY TECHNOLOGY.

WHAT IS THE SEAL OF GOD?

The seal of God, as noted in Isaiah, is contained in His law. Isaiah 8:16 declares: "Seal up the law among my disciples." Thus the focus of the controversy in the last hours of earth's history will center on humanity's response to God's commands. Earth's final issue will be over the seal of God versus the mark of the beast—between God's true sign of authority and Satan's counterfeit.

Government seals may contain three essentials—the name, title, and territory of the ruler and government. The crucial components of God's seal, too, are name, title, and territory—as found in His holy law.

In the very heart of God's ten-commandment law we discover His holy Sabbath. "Remember the Sabbath day by keeping it holy. Six days you shall labor and do all your work, but the seventh day is a Sabbath to the Lord your God. . . . For in six days the Lord made the heavens and the earth, the sea, and all that is in them is, but he rested on the seventh

PHOTODISC

day. Therefore the Lord blessed the Sabbath day and made it holy" (Exodus 20:8-11).

Here in the heart of the Ten Commandments we find God's name ("the Lord your God"), His title (Creator), and His territory (heaven and earth). In this way, the Sabbath can be considered God's seal!

The final battle in the long war between Christ and Satan will center on God's creatorship and rulership. The Sabbath becomes the central issue in the last days. In a very practical way, the beast power has forced the whole world to a test of what has ultimate authority—religious tradition or God's commandments.

THE SEAL OF DIVINE AUTHORITY

God calls the Sabbath His seal, or mark of authority. What does the successor to the medieval church claim as its mark of authority? Reading from its own publications, we find the answer to this crucial question.

The *Catholic Record* of September 1, 1923, puts it this way: "Sunday is our mark of authority. . . . The church is above the Bible, and this transference of sabbath observance is proof of that fact."

And Father T. Enright, one-time C.S.S.R. of Redemptoral College, wrote: "The Bible says, Remember the Sabbath day to keep it holy. The Catholic Church says, 'No. By my divine power I abolish the Sabbath day and command you to keep holy the first day of the week.' And lo! The entire civilized world bows down in a reverent obedience to the command of the holy Catholic Church."

The early church and its successors claimed the authority to shift Christian worship from the Sabbath to another day. But did they have that right? Scripture clearly indicates that even human religious authority cannot do such a thing. Revelation 13:8 predicts that the beast will be the object of worship for everyone except those who have their names written in the book of life belonging to the Lamb, that is, Jesus Christ. Their names will remain in the book of life because they will have maintained their loyalty to God and Jesus, rejecting the mark of the beast and allowing God to seal them with His authority. They will

TEN PROPHETIC SYMBOLS EXPLAINED

	SYMBOL	MEANING	TEXT
1	waters	peoples	Revelation 17:15
2	winds	war, conflict, strife	Jeremiah 49:32
3	beast	king, kingdom	Daniel 7:17, 23
4	pure woman	true church, God's faithful followers	Revelation 12:1; 2 Corinthians 11:2; Ephesians 5:31, 32
5	harlot woman	false religious system	James 4:4
6	blasphemy	claiming equality with God or claiming to forgive sin	John 10:33; Luke 5:21
7	babylon	religious confusion	Revelation 17:5; 18:1-4; Genesis 11:1-7
8	horns	division of, or symbols of, power	Psalm 18:2; Daniel 8:5; 7:21, 24
9	crowns	kingly authority	2 Timothy 4:8; Psalm 21:3; Revelation 19:11-16
10	dragon	Satan or Satan working through pagan Rome	Revelation 12:3, 4, 9

be the redeemed because they have chosen to pledge their allegiance to God, including accepting the seal of His creative power, the Sabbath. It will be a decision of eternal consequences that each person on earth will have to make.

CHAPTER 11

AGENTS OF THE DARK SIDE

Nearly all of us have stood at the graveside of a loved one and said our final goodbyes. Then we've walked away and tried to get on with life, but the silence and emptiness left behind continue to haunt us. We'd give almost anything to hear our loved one's voice just once again—to have the opportunity to reassure them just once more of our love.

And for many, questions intensify that sense of loss. Is there really life after death? Does a person's spirit survive the body and continue on? And if so, can we communicate with our departed loved ones?

In early December of the year 1847 John and Margaret Fox—along with their daughters Catherine and Margaretta—moved into a house in Hydesville, New York, a little town about 20 miles from Rochester. Starting around the middle of March the next spring, the Fox family began to hear strange knocking and rapping sounds each evening, accompanied by the shaking of their beds.

Mrs. Fox in a signed affidavit later described what happened: "On March 30th we were disturbed all night. The noises were heard in all parts of the house. . . . We could not rest, and I then concluded that the house must be haunted by some unhappy restless spirit. I had often heard of such things, but had never witnessed anything of the kind that I could not account for before.

"On Friday night, March 31st, 1848, we concluded to go to bed early and not permit ourselves to be disturbed by the noises, but try and get a night's rest. . . . I had been so broken of my rest I was almost sick. My hus-

RAOUL VITALE

band had not gone to bed when we first heard the noises on this evening. I had just lain down. It commenced as usual. I knew it from all other noises I had ever heard before. The children, who slept in the other bed in the room, heard the rapping, and tried to make similar sounds by snapping their fingers.

"My youngest child, Cathie, said: 'M. Splitfoot, do as I do,' clapping her hands. The sound instantly followed her with the same number of raps. When she stopped, the sound ceased for a short time. Then Margaretta said, in sport, 'Now, do as I do. Count one, two, three, four,' striking one hand against the other at the same time; and the raps came as before."

The Fox sisters worked out a code based on a given number of raps and continued communicating with the spirit young Kate Fox chose to call "Mr. Splitfoot." In time they learned that the spirit claimed that his name was Charles B. Rosna and that he had been a peddler who had stayed at the house five years earlier. He said that he had been murdered and that his body had been buried in the cellar of the house. Digging in the basement found little to confirm the spirit's story. But 56 years later, in 1904, some schoolchildren playing in the cellar discovered an entire human skeleton, not beneath the floor of the cellar, but wedged between the walls and the earth behind it.

What began on a March evening in 1848 historians would later recognize as the birth of modern spiritualism. The Fox sisters went on to make a career of publicly demonstrating their ability to communicate with spirits.

CONTACTING THE DEAD

Today American television programs such as *Beyond With James Van Praagh* and *Crossing Over With John Edward* claim to put audience members in touch with their departed loved ones. And books on the afterlife routinely land on best-seller lists, including, through the years, such titles as *On Life After Death*, by Elisabeth Kubler-Ross; *Life After Life*, by Raymond A. Moody, Jr.; *Life on the Other Side*, by Sylvia Browne;

Embraced by the Light, by Betty J. Eadie; and *We Don't Die*, by Joel Martin and Patricia Romanowski.

Such metaphysical concepts as soul travel, reincarnation, and near-death experiences all depend on a single foundation: accepting that at death the soul, or spirit, survives and lives on. But it's not just practitioners of the paranormal who teach that the soul separates from the body after death. The overwhelming majority of Christian churches and preachers assure grieving survivors that their friends and loved ones have gone to heaven to be with Jesus.

How widespread is this belief? A 2003 survey by the Barna Research Group found that 81 percent of Americans believe in life after death, and that another 9 percent feel that life after death is a possibility but aren't sure.

MOST CHRISTIANS ASSUME THAT THEIR FRIENDS AND LOVED ONES GO STRAIGHT TO HEAVEN AFTER DEATH.

Not long ago an NBC coast-to-coast television program interviewed a group of teenagers, asking them, "Do you believe that the dead can communicate with the living?" The young people answered, "Certainly." In fact, one girl said, "Sure, I do. I frequently see my dead grandmother appearing to me." But can the dead really contact the living? Is there an immortal soul that leaves the body—and can it speak to us at certain times?

J. Arthur Hill, on page 25 of the book *Spiritism: History, Phenomena, and Doctrine*, states that "the fundamental principle in spiritualism is that human beings survive bodily death, and occasionally, under conditions not yet fully understood, we can communicate with those who have gone before." Thus spiritualism argues that when you die, an immortal part of you continues to exist and can even contact the living. It is a concept that many religions, including most Christians, seem to share.

With such overwhelming support for the belief that people live on after death and can still speak to us, how could anyone possibly be so con-

PHOTODISC

trary and foolish as to claim that no soul survives death—that no spirit ascends to God's presence? Yet one voice does challenge the psychics, the channelers, the best sellers, the TV programs, the surveys, and every teacher and preacher of life after death—the voice of God Himself. So let's turn to His own Word, the Bible, and see what He says about the dead communicating with the living.

WHAT HAPPENS WHEN SOMEBODY DIES?

According to Scripture, any voice that breaks death's silence does not come from God. The dead cannot return and communicate with the living. "As a cloud vanishes and is gone, so he who goes down to the grave does not return. He will never come to his house again; his place will know him no more" (Job 7:9, 10).

Could it be any plainer? A person who dies can no longer return to his or her earthly home. Job cries out in Job 14:12-15, "So man lies down and does not rise; till the heavens are no more, men will not awake or be roused from their sleep. If only you would hide me in the grave and conceal me till your anger has passed! If only you would set me a time and then remember me! If a man dies, will he live again? All the days of my hard service I will wait for my renewal to come. You will call and I will answer you; you will long for the creature your hands have made."

In clear, unmistakable language Job describes death as a sleep until resurrection morning. This is why he says, "Only a few years will pass before I go on the journey of no return" (Job 16:22). Yet he later adds, "I know that my Redeemer lives, and that in the end he will stand upon the earth. And after my skin has been destroyed, yet in my flesh I will see God" (Job 19:25, 26).

The patriarchs, prophets, apostles, and all true believers

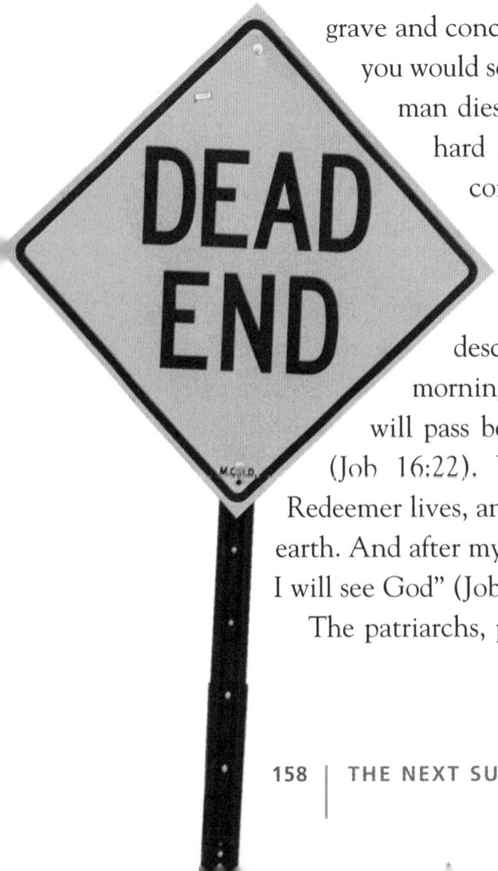

GOD'S WORD CONDEMNS THE OCCULT, SPIRITUALISM, FORTUNETELLERS, AND ALL FORMS OF ATTEMPTED COMMUNICATION WITH THE DEAD

1	Leviticus 19:31	"Do not turn to mediums or seek out spiritists, for you will be defiled by them."
2	Leviticus 20:27	"A man or woman who is a medium or spiritist . . . must be put to death." In ancient Israel God did not tolerate spiritualism.
3	Deuteronomy 18:10,11	"Let no one be found among you . . . who is a medium or spiritist. . . . Anyone who does these things is detestable to the Lord."
4	1 Samuel 28:3	"Saul had expelled the mediums and spiritists from the land."
5	Isaiah 8:19, 20	"When men tell you to consult mediums and spiritists, . . . should not a people inquire of their God?"
6	Isaiah 47:14	"Surely [your astrologers] are like stubble. . . . They cannot even save themselves."
7	Jeremiah 27:9	"Do not listen . . . to your mediums or your sorcerers."
8	Malachi 3:5	"I [God] will be quick to testify against sorcerers."
9	Revelation 21:8	"Those who practice magic arts . . . —their place will be in the fiery lake of burning sulfur."
10	Revelation 22:15	"Outside [the New Jerusalem] are . . . those who practice magic arts."

PHOTODISC

in Bible times looked forward to seeing their Lord when He came to our earth in glory. But they did not anticipate an immediate leap into His presence at death. They rejected the unbiblical notion of the immortal soul taught by the pagan religions around them.

Remember Satan's first lie repeated to Eve in Genesis 3:4: "You will not surely die"? The pages of best-selling books and supermarket tabloids constantly repeat that lie. It echoes from the pulpits of countless churches. Television presents it as a fact as spiritualist mediums claim to contact departed loved ones on the "other side." And American movies such as *Ghost*, *Poltergeist*, and scores of others popularize it.

GETTING INVOLVED WITH THE SUPERNATURAL IS FORBIDDEN BY GOD AND SPIRITUALLY DANGEROUS.

The Bible says in Romans 6:23 that "the wages of sin is death." But Satan lied and said, "No, you can sin and you won't die, because you have an immortal soul that lives on. Not even God can destroy it." Always remember that Satan is the father of lies (John 8:44)—and that the first lie he told to Eve had to do with death.

The spiritualist even goes so far as to say that Satan is not a liar—that he told the truth. Here spiritualist E. W. Sprague even quotes the Bible when he declares: "Spiritualism says that the dead know more than the living. 'And the serpent said unto the woman, "You shall not surely die."' Genesis 3:4. In this, as in many other Bible passages, the Devil told the truth and the Lord is in error."

No, the devil did not tell the truth—and the Lord is not in error! If the Lord said in Genesis 2:17, "You will surely die," then you will do exactly that.

Today, many accept mediums and channelers as having superior spiritual gifts—as being especially blessed by God. But notice what He says about them in Leviticus 20:27: "A man or a woman who is a medium or spiritist among you must be put to death." And notice, too, what God says in Deuteronomy 18:10-12: "Let no one be found among you who sacrifices his son or daughter in the fire, who practices divination or sorcery, interprets omens, engages in witchcraft, or casts spells, or who is a medium or spiritist or who consults the dead. Anyone who does these things is detestable to the Lord, and because of these detestable practices the Lord your God will drive out those nations before you."

Now, why would God issue such strong prohibitions against those who might put us in touch with the dead? Why does God forbid us to consult our departed loved ones, if they're really alive and can talk to us? Couldn't we gain much comfort and wisdom from talking to a loving parent or other relative who now dwells in the very presence of God? After all, God loves us, and Psalm 84:11 assures us: "The Lord bestores favor and honor; no good thing does he withhold from those whose walk is blameless."

"WHY CONSULT THE DEAD ON BEHALF OF THE LIVING?" (ISAIAH 8:19).

So why, then, does He withhold from us any contact with beings who claim to be our loved ones? Because God knows that the supposed spirits of the dead are really spirits of the enemy—devils and demons!

Spiritualism is not something to play with. Whatever your emotions may tell you, any form that might materialize is not your wife, your son, your daughter, or any other human being. However sincere and convincing the words of a medium may sound on a TV show—or the words in a book on the afterlife—that can't and won't and don't change what God has said.

In Isaiah 8:20 God flatly stated: "To the law and to the testimony! If they do not speak according to this word, they have no light of dawn." The Word of God is the standard by which we are to test truth. Isaiah 8:19 declares: "When men tell you to consult mediums and spiritists, who whisper and mutter, should not a people inquire of their God? Why consult the dead on behalf of the living?"

The Bible says, "Don't go seeking knowledge about the dead from some spiritualistic sources. Instead, seek God. Find out what the Bible says about death."

In the next chapter, "The Lie at the End of the Tunnel," we will explore in depth what the Bible says about death. But in this chapter I would like to note three clear biblical facts:

- Spiritualism, which is deeply rooted in the idea of the immortal soul, is deadly.
- God's power is greater than all the evil forces of Satan.
- The final victory over Satan and evil and death will be at the return of Jesus.

SPIRITUALISM IS DEADLY

God had marvelous plans for Saul, the first king of Israel. But his life illustrates the tragic result of rejecting divine counsel. Although the Lord spared Saul's life on numerous occasions, the apostate king continued in rebellion against Him. He rejected God's Word through the prophet Samuel. Scripture records that "the Spirit of the Lord had departed from Saul, and an evil spirit . . . tormented him" (1 Samuel 16:14). In his own rebellious way Saul sought guidance from the Lord, but "the Lord did not answer him" (1 Samuel 28:6).

His spiritual emptiness plunged him into deep depression. King Saul did not know what to do. Eventually, as a last resort, he contacted a spirit medium. As ruler of Israel, Saul knew about the condemnation of mediums that God had given through Moses: "Anyone who does these things is detestable to the Lord, and because of these detestable practices the Lord your God will drive out those nations before you" (Deuteronomy 18:12).

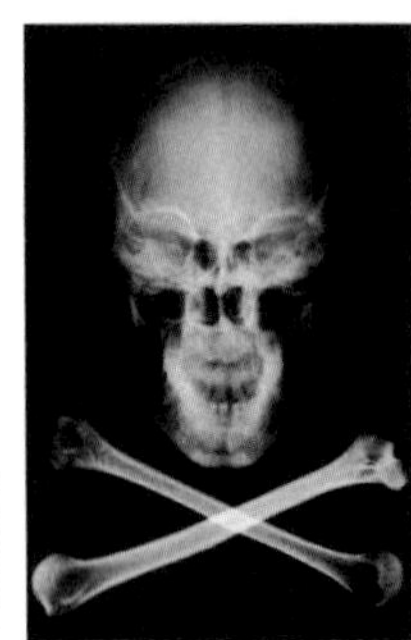
PHOTODISC

Yet in spite of clear divine instruction, Saul consulted the medium. When Samuel, his spiritual mentor, had been alive, the king had rejected the prophet's godly counsel, but now he wanted to have

PHOTODISC

a witch bring Samuel back from the dead so that he could listen to the voice he had ignored previously. Disguising himself, Saul consulted a witch. But would God speak through a witch to answer Saul? Certainly not! The woman recognized the king, and, fearful that he would put her to death based on God's command, she refused to intervene with the spirit world. But, assuring her of her safety, Saul urged her to bring Samuel back from the dead. Soon the witch saw a "spirit coming up out of the ground" (1 Samuel 28:13). The king was sure that it must be Samuel (verse 14).

SCRIPTURE DECLARES THAT THE LIVING CANNOT CONTACT THE DEAD FOR HELP, COMFORT, OR KNOWLEDGE.

The message Saul received, however, sent him into an even deeper depression. Rather than repent before God, he accepted defeat as inevitable. And rather than seek God's mercy, Saul wept in despair. The next day with his armies defeated in battle, the king took his own life with his sword. Spiritualism is deadly. It destroys the lives of all who play with it.

Satan is a brilliant though fallen angel, full of deception. The apostle Paul stated it well to the Ephesian Christians when he said, "For our struggle is not against flesh and blood, but against the rulers, against the authorities, against the powers of this dark world and against the spiritual forces of evil in the heavenly realms" (Ephesians 6:12).

As we have seen repeatedly in this book, a spiritual warfare wages in the universe. Good and evil struggle for control. But the Bible leaves no doubt that Jesus is stronger than all the forces of hell. He is more powerful than all the evil angels combined. Although the "devil prowls around like a roaring lion looking for someone to devour" (1 Peter 5:8), we have the assurance that "the one who is in you is greater than the one who is in the world" (1 John 4:4).

Satan may triumph in some battles here. He may appear to be winning the war, but the book of Revelation presents the good news that Jesus will ultimately, finally, completely, and totally win. God will vanquish Satan and his evil angels forever. The forces of hell "will make war against the Lamb, but the Lamb will overcome them because he is Lord of lords and King of kings" (Revelation 17:14).

Revelation 19 pictures Jesus symbolically riding on a white horse, galloping triumphantly through the heavens. On His robe is written "King of kings and Lord of lords" (Revelation 19:16). Our coming King, our conquering General, our victorious Lord, destroys the forces of hell once and for all. As the apostle Paul triumphantly exclaimed: "Then the saying that is written will come true: 'Death has been swallowed up in victory'" (1 Corinthians 15:54).

Believers down through the centuries have looked forward to the return of our Lord as the great day of victory celebration. They have longed for the second com-

As the apostle Paul awaited death in the Mamertine Prison, which used to exist on this site, he clung to his hope in Jesus' second coming and the resurrection of the righteous.

Siegfried Horn Museum

ing of Christ to vanquish death. Instead of expecting eternal life at the moment of death, they have anticipated triumph over death at the return of our Lord. The second coming of Christ was their "blessed hope" (Titus 2:13).

Dying in a dungeon in Rome, the apostle Paul clutched the hope of the Advent. Writing to his young disciple, Timothy, he confidently exclaimed, "I have fought the good fight, I have finished the race, I have kept the faith. Now there is in store for me the crown of righteousness, which the Lord, the righteous Judge, will award to me on that day—and not only to me, but also to all who have longed for his appearing" (2 Timothy 4:7, 8).

At the second coming of Christ we will be reunited with our faithful believing loved ones again.

The imprisoned apostle did not believe that he would immediately enter the presence of God. Nor did he think that some inherent and immortal soul would wing its way to worlds afar at death. Instead he eagerly looked forward to the glorious return of our Lord to defeat all evil forces and usher in eternity.

God has something much better than the voices of evil spirits pretending to be our loved ones. At the second coming of Christ we will embrace our faithful, believing loved ones again. Then we will hear not the voices of evil spirits but the real voices of our loved ones. They will not be some vague, shadowy form perhaps hovering above us in a dark room. Instead we will ascend into the heavens with them, surrounded by the glory of God in our resurrected bodies.

This is our hope, our destiny. It is something worth holding on to.

Rubberball

CHAPTER 12

THE LIE AT THE END OF THE TUNNEL

Though some details differ, the descriptions provided by many who say they've had a near-death experience appear remarkably similar. A man we'll call Harry is lying in a hospital bed as doctors work feverishly to restart his heart. Soon Harry feels himself leaving his body and rising from the bed to hover near the ceiling. He looks down at himself, watching as the physicians continue their efforts until all hope is gone and they pronounce him dead.

Then Harry notices some kind of tunnel forming near him. The tunnel moves toward him and envelops him. Suddenly he finds himself moving through it at great speed—heading toward a light at the other end that grows larger and brighter. The light transforms into a radiant being, and Harry feels the force of a love too profound for words.

Stories like our fictional Harry's have become all too common today. Some of the world's best-selling books explore such near-death experiences. Take the case of Betty J. Eadie, for example.

One evening in 1973, following surgery, Betty rested in her hospital bed. After drifting off to sleep, she suddenly awakened. Soon she sensed herself leaving her body and then found herself traveling at high speed through a dark, warm mass of some kind. Here's how she described it in her 1992 best-selling book entitled *Embraced by the Light*.

"I saw a pinpoint of light in the distance. The black mass around me began to take on more of the shape of a tunnel, and I felt myself traveling through it at an even greater speed, rushing toward the light. . . . As

RAOUL VITALE

PHOTODISC

I approached it, I noticed the figure of a man standing in it, with the light radiating all around him. As I got closer the light became brilliant—brilliant beyond description, far more brilliant than the sun. . . .

"Although his light was much brighter than my own, I was aware that my light, too, illuminated us. And as our lights merged, I felt as if I had stepped into his countenance, and I felt an utter explosion of love.

MANY HAVE REPORTED HAVING NEAR-DEATH EXPERIENCES DURING MEDICAL EMERGENCIES.

"It was the most unconditional love I have ever felt, and as I saw his arms open to receive me I went to him and received his complete embrace and said over and over, 'I'm home. I'm home. I'm finally home.'"

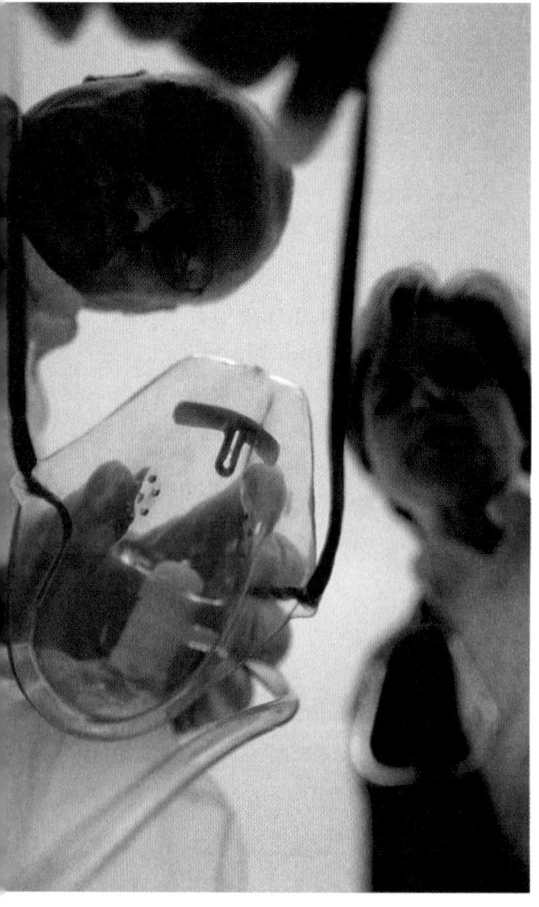

Is it true that when we die we leave our bodies and travel toward a light? A light that turns out to be God, waiting to welcome us home?

Those who write of near-death experiences assure us that while at death the body may perish, the conscious soul still lives on. And thousands of preachers in pulpits around the world present similar messages. It has become accepted belief that losing someone in death means that that person has gone to heaven to be with Jesus. People just assume that their loved ones are up there looking down on them as they continue living here on earth.

But popular opinion does not decide the truth about what happens at death. It's not decided by what best-selling authors claim to know or by what any church teaches or by the attempts of a television medium to contact spirits during prime time. Nor is it determined by you or me. Only God can confirm the truth about death—or anything else. And if God says something is true, a thousand or a million voices raised against it don't make it false, just as a thousand or a million voices repeating a lie don't make it true.

PHOTODISC

PEOPLE HAVING NEAR-DEATH EXPERIENCES OFTEN REPORT SEEING A BRIGHT LIGHT.

So it's vital that we know God's truth about death. And for that, once again we need to go all the way back to the very beginning—to our original human parents, Adam and Eve, in the Garden of Eden.

As you will remember, when God created our world and the first human beings, He placed them in the perfect Garden of Eden. There He warned them about a tree located in the center of the garden. "You are free to eat from any tree in the garden; but you must not eat from the tree of the knowledge of good and evil, for when you eat of it you will surely die" (Genesis 2:16, 17).

It was not long after this that Eve—and then Adam—made a tragic decision to ignore the divine caution. Eve wandered near the forbidden tree, and there in its branches, disguised as a talking serpent, was Satan himself. As we saw earlier, God had to cast him out of heaven because of rebellion. And now, on this perfect world, the evil one determined to lure Adam and Eve into turning against God as well. From his place in the tree Satan said to the woman, " 'Did God really say, "You must not eat from any tree in the garden"?'

"The woman said to the serpent, 'We may eat fruit from the trees in the garden, but God did say, "You must not eat fruit from the tree that is in the middle of the garden, and you must not touch it, or you will die." '

" 'You will surely not die,' the serpent said to the woman. 'For God knows that when you eat of it your eyes will be opened, and you will be like God, knowing good and evil' " (Genesis 3:1-5).

PHOTODISC

God said, "You will die."

But Satan said, "You will *not* surely die."

Thus the first lie on earth had to do with death. It's the same one repeated freely and so convincingly today by authors, mediums, and even preachers. There is no death, it claims. A time comes when an immortal soul simply leaves our body and enters a higher plain of existence—when we are embraced by the light. But the Bible declares, "The wages of sin is death" (Romans 6:23). And death is the absence of life.

In the Garden of Eden God did not say to our first parents, "If you eat of the tree of knowledge of good and evil, you will enter into an eternal state of immortality." Instead, He declared very plainly, "You will die."

ISN'T THE SOUL IMMORTAL?

Here is what the Bible teaches about immortality.

- Only God is immortal (1 Timothy 6:16).
- Human beings in our current condition are mortal (Job 4:17).
- We seek immortality (Romans 2:7).
- We will receive immortality when Jesus comes again (1 Thessalonians 4:16, 17; 1 Corinthians 15:51-57).

PHOTODISC

The Bible uses the word "soul" 1,600 times, but never once does Scripture speak of an immortal soul, an undying soul, an everlasting soul, or an eternal soul. Such a concept has another source. Beware of that lie, for it comes from the one the Bible in John 8:44 calls the father of lies.

But, you may wonder, if we don't leave our bodies at death—if we don't live on and go to heaven—then what *does* happen to us when we die? Centuries ago Job asked the question that every person faces sometime during his or her life: "If a man dies, will he live again?" (Job 14:14).

ISLAM (LEFT), BUDDHISM (ABOVE), AND HINDUISM (BELOW), LIKE ALL RELIGIONS, HAVE A BELIEF IN THE AFTERLIFE IN WHICH PEOPLE RECEIVE REWARDS OR PUNISHMENTS FOR HOW THEY LIVED IN THIS LIFE.

PHOTODISC

Religious people have offered an array of answers to what happens after death. For example, Muslims believe that a person's ultimate destination is either heaven ("garden of Allah"), which is described in delightful materialistic language, or hell, which has many tortures that are depicted by graphic images. Hindus regard death as a great journey, in which one goes through cycles of reincarnation with many levels of existence—upper ones of light and lower ones of darkness. They consider that only the body dies, never the soul. The immortal soul—*atman*—constitutes what one really is. However, no one abides permanently in these stages of existence. The ultimate goal is to become nothing by entering the abyss of Brahman. Buddhists teach an ultimate Nirvana, which is more a state of blissful liberation than a physical place. Shintoists conceive of a staircase—*Ama-No-Hashidate*—that links earth with the afterlife. Australian Aborigines look forward to the soul being ferried upstream to *braigu*, where they are united with long-deceased kin.

Many Inuits think that at death the good souls go to "the land of the moon," where they enjoy blissful rest forever. But the bad souls travel to *Adlivun*, which is at the bottom of the sea, where it's forever dark and cold.

Even within Christianity itself, interpretations about an afterlife vary. Many would have us believe that immediately after death a person must "face the music"—and go either "up" or "down"! Others teach that those who have died have entered into a sleep, resting until the return of Jesus to this earth.

The book of Isaiah assures us: "Your dead will live; their bodies will rise. You who dwell in dust, wake up and shout for joy" (Isaiah 26:19). Yes, the Bible promises a life beyond death! Our beloved dead will live again. But when? At the time of death—or at some later time? Again, what, exactly, happens when a person dies?

The Bible's teaching on death is consistent. As we study it we may encounter some surprises, but it is both reasonable and satisfying—and best of all, comforting.

One of the most-quoted passages of Scripture concerning death appears in Ecclesiastes 12:7: "The dust returns to the ground it came from, and the spirit returns to God who gave it." But what is it exactly that returns to the Lord? Here's where people make a mistake. They don't understand what the "spirit" is. For example, is it conscious and able to think? The Hebrew word *ruach*, translated "spirit," comes from the same root as other words pertaining to "breath" or "breathing," such as "inspire" or "respiration."

THROUGHOUT THE BIBLE, A PERSON'S SPIRIT IS DEFINED AS THE BREATH OF LIFE.

The New Testament Greek word often rendered "spirit" is *pneuma*, which provides the root for such words as "pneumonia," the respiratory disease, and "pneumatic," a description for tires that we blow up with air.

But let's listen to the Bible define what the spirit that goes back to God is. Hebrew poetry as we find in the Old Testament has a literary device called *parallelism*, in which the first phrase says something and the second phrase echoes it in a different way. Thus the two lines mean the same thing but use different words. For example, Job tells us what the spirit of God is: "All the while my breath is in me, and the spirit of God is in my nostrils" (Job 27:3, KJV).

SCRIPTURE CONSISTENTLY REFERS TO DEATH AS SLEEP

Speaking of the death of kings and other individuals, the books of 1 Kings and 2 Kings as well as 2 Chronicles use the expression "he slept [died] with his fathers" 37 times.

So the spirit is equal to, or the same as, the breath. God breathed into humanity the breath of life. In other words, God put into us His life-giving spirit. When a person dies, what goes back to God? The breath of God—the spark of life—returns to Him.

OUR BODIES RETURN TO DUST

When we die, our bodies—made up of the basic physical elements of the earth—decay into dust, and the spirit, or breath or life, returns to God. In order to understand fully what the Bible writer means by "spirit," let's take a look at the very first book of the Bible and watch in Genesis 2:7 as God created humanity: "The Lord God formed the man from the dust of the ground and breathed into his nostrils the breath of life, and the man became a living being ["soul" (KJV)]."

God took the elements of the earth: carbon, hydrogen, oxygen, nitrogen, calcium, iron, phosphorous, sodium, and other substances, and formed the body. Adam then had a brain, but he was not yet thinking. He had a heart in his chest, but it was not yet beating. Blood filled his arteries and veins, but it did not yet circulate. The first man was ready to live, but life had not yet entered his body.

Now watch as God tenderly bent over him and breathed into his nostrils the breath of life. As the Lord did so, a miraculous process that no modern scientist has ever been able to duplicate occurred—a physical human became a living soul! Or, as the New International Version of the Bible puts it, "the man became a living being."

Thus the breath, or spirit, is life's spark—the spirit, or breath, distinguishes a live person from a dead one! The apostle James refers to this life force as the "spirit": "The body without the spirit is dead" (James 2:26).

Simply put, the Bible equation is: DUST + SPIRIT = LIVING SOUL. Or to put it even more clearly: THE PHYSICAL ELEMENTS OF EARTH + BREATH = LIVING BEING.

If this is the process of life, then, what happens at death? Just the reverse: DUST — SPIRIT = CORPSE. Or, more simply: ELEMENTS OF EARTH — BREATH = CORPSE.

We can best understand this truth by the following illustration. When you connect a light bulb to electricity, what happens? You get light. No one "puts" the light into the bulb. The light comes on by the uniting of the two components: bulb + electricity. When you disconnect the electricity, the light goes out. Just so at death. When the breath, or spark of life, goes back to the Creator, a person dies. All that remains is the body, composed of the various elements, which then decays into dust. The living soul, or living being, simply ceases to exist.

The pagan Greeks—especially the philosopher Plato—asserted that the human soul is "imperishable." The Egyptians, Babylonians, and Persians before them all developed elaborate systems for worshipping the dead because they believed the doctrine of the immortal soul. (But even the Egyptians assumed that people could cease to exist altogether if they did not pass the judgment each person had to face in the afterlife. They called that eternal destruction the "second death.")

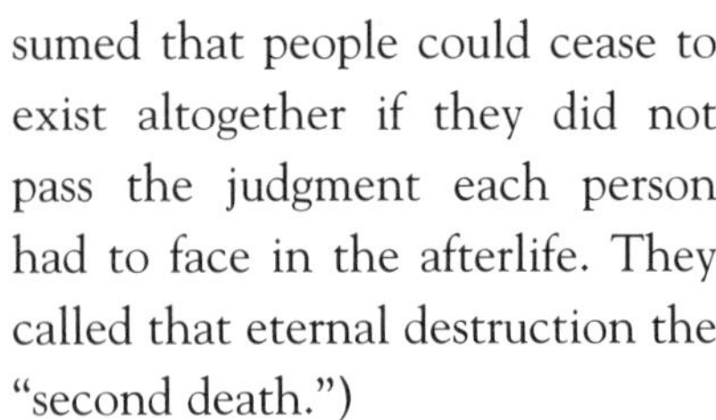

THE EGYPTIANS BELIEVED THEIR GOD ANUBES WEIGHED EACH PERSON'S HEART TO SEE IF THEY WOULD LIVE FOREVER OR BE DESTROYED ETERNALLY.

In Scripture the word "soul" has two meanings.

First, the Bible sometimes uses it to describe a living person. This is the case in both Genesis 2:7 and Ezekiel 18:4. God breathed into man the breath of life, and he became a "living soul" (KJV), or a living person. "The soul [or person] who sins is the one who will die."

Second, the Bible word "soul" may also mean life. For instance, Jesus taught that "whosoever will save his life shall lose it: and whosoever will lose his life for my sake shall find it. For what is a man profited, if he shall gain the whole world, and lose his own soul? or what shall a man give in exchange for his soul?" (Matthew 16:25, 26, KJV). In this passage Matthew employed the same Greek word—*psyche*—four times, but the King James Version translates it twice as "life" and twice as "soul." The two words are interchangeable. Life is not something irrevocably ours. We can lose it.

THE IMMORTAL SOUL IS ONE OF THE GREATEST MISUNDERSTANDINGS OF CHRISTIANITY

"If we were to ask an ordinary Christian today (whether well-read Protestant or Catholic, or not) what he conceived to be the New Testament teaching concerning the fate of man after death, with few exceptions we should get the answer: 'The immortality of the soul.' Yet this widely-accepted idea is one of the greatest misunderstandings of Christianity" (Oscar Cullman, *Immortality of the Soul or Resurrection of the Dead?* [New York: MacMillan, 1964], p. 15).

"Mortal" means subject to death and "immortal" the opposite—imperishable. As we have already noted, you do not find "immortal soul" or the idea of the soul's inherent immortality even once in the Bible. God's Word does not teach such a concept. But we do have the promise of immortality—received by the faithful as a gift when Jesus returns.

Paul writes, "I tell you a mystery: We will not all sleep, but we will all be changed—in a flash, in the twinkling of an eye, at the last trumpet. . . . For the perishable must clothe itself with the imperishable, and the mortal with immortality" (1 Corinthians 15:51-53).

We mortals, who are subject to death and decay, must put on immortality at Christ's second coming. At death we do not go directly to heaven or hell because we have some so-called inherent immortal soul.

The Bible states in Psalm 146:3, 4: "Do not put your trust in princes, in mortal men, who cannot save. When their spirit departs, they return to the ground; on that very day their plans come to nothing." But where do the dead spend their time between death and the resurrection? Job clearly tells us: "If I wait, the grave is mine house" (Job 17:13, KJV).

According to the Bible, when people die they do not go to heaven, hell, or purgatory. In fact, they do not live at all—anywhere! Death is a cessation of life until the resurrection morning, when God will reunite body and breath again. Notice Ecclesiastes 9:5: "For the living know that they will die, but the dead know nothing." Nothing! Zero! Clearly the dead have no awareness of what happens among the living, for the Bible says in Job 14:21 of the man who has died: "If his sons are honored, he does not know it; if they are brought low, he does not see it."

CORBIS

Isn't that the best way, after all, if you think about it? Imagine a young mother dying and going directly to heaven, leaving behind a husband and several small children. From her place in glory the young woman looks down and sees all that is happening on earth. Let's suppose that her husband begins to drink heavily and beats the children. Further, he has a live-in girlfriend who cruelly neglects the children.

Because Scripture says that the dead are not aware of anything, a mother would be spared any tragedy that may happen to those she leaves behind.

Day after day the young woman watches the scene below, appalled at the situation but helpless to do anything about it. How would you describe the daily horror that she would feel? She has no relief, day or night! Wouldn't heaven be hell for her? Or what about parents who would see their children blown apart in the ravages of war?

JESUS CALLED DEATH A SLEEP

Matthew 9:24	"The girl is not dead but asleep."
Mark 5:39	"The child is not dead but asleep."
Luke 8:52	"She is not dead but asleep."
John 11:11, 14	"Our friend Lazarus has fallen asleep. Lazarus is dead."

Each of the four Gospel writers—Matthew, Mark, Luke, and John—clearly understood our Lord's teaching that death is a sleep until the resurrection.

One of the most comforting truths in God's Word is that when we die, we rest quietly, undisturbed by the problems of life or by concern for loved ones until the call of the Life-giver. Is it any wonder that the Bible compares death to a sleep?

The story of Lazarus reveals many insights into the biblical view of death. In speaking of the demise of His close friend, Jesus Himself called death a "sleep." He told His disciples, "Our friend Lazarus has fallen asleep; but I am going there to wake him up" (John 11:11).

DEATH IS A SLEEP

The disciples, knowing that Lazarus had been ill for some time, replied, "'Lord, if he sleeps, he will get better.' Jesus had been speaking of his death, but his disciples thought that he meant natural sleep. So then he told them plainly, 'Lazarus is dead'" (verses 12-14).

Lazarus sleeps, Jesus said.

Yes, Lazarus is dead. But he sleeps.

Then Jesus went on to perform a miracle that only God could possibly accomplish. He called Lazarus back to life!

Imagine the impact on the crowd as Lazarus did indeed come forth, wrapped in the same graveclothes he had been buried in. Although he had been dead for four days, the Bible gives no record of Lazarus recounting any experiences from during that time. How could he, if the "dead know nothing"? Jesus had simply brought him back from the sleep of death—a sleep that can be broken only by the summons of the Life-giver Himself!

What a wonderful hope Christians have of a life beyond the grave! In the tombs of the catacombs of Rome, we find the inscriptions of those who died in pagan hopelessness. Again and again we see inscribed words of sorrow and finality: "Goodbye for all eternity." "Goodbye forever." Yet on the tombs of early Christians appear words of hope and courage: "Goodbye until we meet again." "Good night until the morning."

No, Christians need not sorrow and grieve in utter despair like those who have no hope of being reunited with their loved ones. The apostle Paul told the early Christians in 1 Thessalonians 4:13: "We do not want you to be ignorant about those who fall asleep, or to grieve like the rest of men, who have no hope."

The real comfort for sorrowing, grieving hearts does not exist in the séance chamber or in the confused messages of a New Age channeler. Nor do we find it in the claims of an author about some near-death experience. Our real hope is in Jesus Christ. And equally important, our only security from demonic deception is in His Word.

The book of Revelation unfolds Satan's master plan to delude multitudes in the last days through spiritualism, based on Satan's lie that the soul is immortal. Writing from the rocky, barren island of Patmos, John declared, "They are spirits of demons performing miraculous signs, and they go out to the kings of the whole world, to gather them for the battle on the great day of God Almighty" (Revelation 16:14).

The devil's final deception revolves around evil angels impersonating the dead to deceive political leaders. Revelation 18:23 adds, "By your magic spell all the nations were led astray." Seeing is not always believing. Isn't it just like the father of lies to take advantage of our grief at the death of a loved one and impersonate the dead?

THE CASE OF THE MISPLACED COMMA

Scripture tells us to follow the teachings of Jesus. But what did Jesus Himself teach about death? People constantly ask me about the thief on the cross. What did Jesus mean when He spoke to him and promised that "today you will be with me in paradise" (Luke 23:43)?

Did He mean that the thief would go with Him to Paradise that very day? Obviously not, because when Mary came to Jesus on the resurrection morning, she looked at Jesus through her tears and thought He was the gardener. After Jesus revealed Himself, Mary threw herself at His feet. Then Jesus said: "Do not hold on to me, for I have not yet returned to the Father" (John 20:17).

JESUS DID NOT PROMISE THE THIEF THAT HE WOULD IMMEDIATELY GO TO HEAVEN.

Jesus' promise to the thief appears, on the surface in certain English translations, to present a strange contradiction. First, it seems to contradict the clear Bible teaching on the subject of death—that a person sleeps in the grave until called forth by Jesus. Second, if Jesus had not yet

Jesus told Mary that He had not yet gone to His Father.

ascended to His Father on Sunday morning, how could He have told the thief on Friday that they'd be in Paradise together that same day? Are we forced to believe either Christ's statement to Mary on Sunday morning or His promise to the thief on Friday afternoon?

When we encounter an apparent contradiction in the Bible, we immediately realize that something is wrong—not with the Word of God, but with our limited understanding or with the translation.

But this particular apparent contradiction instantly disappears with the simple movement of a comma. The placement of a comma can make a world of difference. We must remember that the punctuation found in the Bible is *not* inspired. In fact, the original Greek New Testament manuscripts had *no* punctuation at all!

Different forms of punctuation were added at different times. Even when the King James Version appeared in 1611 with some punctuation, it still had no quotation marks around words spoken. Later versions supplied them. Besides not using modern punctuation, the ancient manuscripts ran all the words together—either in all uppercase or all lowercase letters—like this: THISISWHATANCIENTGREEKLOOKEDLIKE-OFCOURSEITISNTGREEKITSENGLISHBUTYOUGETTHEPOINT. In many ways you had to know what a text already said to be able to read it. As a result, those who added the commas and other punctuation marks to Scripture had no help from Luke's Greek manuscript, because the Greek was written with no breaks between sentences or even words, perhaps in order to save on costly parchments.

So the comma in this verse did not get supplied until many centuries

Russell Harlan

after Luke wrote. Translators used their best judgment in inserting punctuation, but they were certainly not inspired. If their mistaken belief in the immortality of the soul colored their interpretation of the text, they would naturally put the comma in the wrong place, which is exactly what happened.

We can place the comma in our text either before or after the word "today." Where the comma is placed depends on someone's personal choice: "Truly, I say to you, today you will be with me in Paradise" (Luke 23:43, RSV). "Truly, I say to you today, you will be with me in Paradise."

WHAT JESUS REALLY SAID TO THE THIEF

What did Jesus really say to the thief? It's very simple. He boldly made this promise—"*Today*, as I die on the cross and My ministry ends in agony and shame; *today*, as blood runs down My face and nails pierce My hands; *today*, when it doesn't look as if I can save anyone and My claim to be the Son of God appears false; *today*, when My own disciples have forsaken Me; *today*, in My darkest hour, you understand who I am; and I assure you *today*, despite how things seem to look, you will be with Me in Paradise."

The Bible is plain that Jesus Himself did not go to Paradise on that day. On that Friday, instead, Christ would enter the grave and rest in the tomb. And as the Bible says, He did not ascend to His Father until some time after encountering Mary Magdalene on Sunday morning. All conflict and contradiction disappear when we place the comma properly.

Because Christ burst the bonds of the tomb—because He went into the grave and came out triumphant—you and I need not fear death. Paul sings: "'Where, O death, is your sting?' . . . Thanks be to God! He gives us the victory through our Lord Jesus Christ" (1 Corinthians 15:55-57). Christ Himself removed the tragic sting from death and gave us victory over the tomb.

THE REVELATION

CHAPTER 13

IS THE UNITED STATES THE FINAL SUPERPOWER?

The vote was deadlocked on July 2, 1776. Should the band of British colonies declare their independence from England? The Continental Congress debated all that day. The Delaware delegation had three votes. Of the two delegates present, one voted for independence. The other opposed it. The third delegate was at home on his farm, marooned there because of a heavy rainstorm. But he received word that the congress had reached an impasse. And his vote might decide the future. And so on horseback he rode all night through the mud and rain to the Continental Congress to cast the deciding vote.

Legend has it that a little boy watched the delegates through the crack in the door. His grandfather had assigned him the task, because the grandfather was the local bell ringer. And the old man waited at the bell tower, ready to ring the bell if the assembly signed the declaration. As the lad looked through the door, he saw quill pens signing the document and heard the shuffling of feet. The grandfather kept walking back and forth, muttering that they would never approve it.

But then the delegate from Delaware arrived to cast the deciding vote. The little boy ran over and shouted, "Ring, Grandpa, ring for liberty."

The United States has always pictured itself as the place that cherishes liberty. It has become a stronghold of democracy in the modern world. In fact, the nation has become the dominant world power. The issues of liberty and human conscience loom large in the end-time drama that the biblical book of Revelation highlights. Will the United States

PROPHECY SETS THE STAGE FOR THE APPEARANCE OF A NEW BEAST—ONE EMERGING FROM THE LAND INSTEAD OF THE SEA.

still be ringing the liberty bell in the last days?

Perhaps it does. Look at Revelations 13:11. John has just pictured the rise of the medieval church, the papal power, and predicted its role in the end-times. Now he introduces a second prophetic symbol: "Then I saw another beast, coming out of the earth. He had two horns like a lamb." What clues do we have to identify this lamblike beast?

CLUE 1: *Where* this beast arises. The second beast, separate and distinct from the first, arises from the *earth*.

As we saw previously, Daniel 7:17 reveals that prophetic beasts represent kingdoms or nations. So this second beast in Revelation 13 is a nation. And it develops out of the earth. Now, where did the first beast of Revelation 13 come from? It had its origin in the sea. All the other beasts (that is, nations) that we have studied had a similar origin.

Remember, Revelation 17:15 indicates that the sea symbol represents peoples, nations, and tongues—tumultuous masses of people. As an apocalyptic symbol, the sea had a negative connotation, and the nations that arose from it opposed God and His chosen people. (Interestingly,

HARRY BAERG

Revelation 21:1 tells us that the world to come will have no sea.) But this second beast (nation) of Revelation 13:11 arises from the earth—unique in apocalyptic predictions. In the book of Revelation the earth, the opposite of the sea, has a positive connotation. In fact, in Revelation 12:16, the earth helps the persecuted woman (symbol of God's people) by swallowing the deluge that the satanic dragon spewed out in an attempt to drown it. This beast (nation) from the earth, unlike the beasts (nations) from the sea, is on God's side!

Clue 2: The time period of the origin for the second beast. Revelation 13:10 describes the first beast as going "into captivity." Then the very next verse speaks of the rise of the second beast. The second beast (nation) thus came into being about the same time as the first beast went into captivity, the time it received that wound in its head (verse 3).

In the previois chapter we learned that the first beast, the Papacy, received a serious wound in 1798. That's when the French took the pope prisoner, breaking the political supremacy of the Papacy. The second prophetic beast began to gain prominence after this time. Does that fit the history of the United States? Yes, it does. In 1798 the new country was gaining a reputation as a nation to be reckoned with. Thus when we scan history, we discover that only one world power was "arising" in 1798—the United States of America.

Clue 3: How this second beast rose up. Revelation 13:11 tells us that it had two horns like a lamb. What significance do they have? As we learned earlier, Scripture uses horns as a symbol of authority or power. The lamb is young, with only a little apparent power. Furthermore, Revelation uses the lamb to symbolize Jesus Christ nearly 30 times. Here is another indication that this beast (nation) is not an enemy of God and His people.

Clue 4: Previous beasts had crowns on their horns. Crowns indicate kingly power in prophecy. But here we see no sign of kingly authority, in contrast to the first beast in Revelation 13. "I saw a beast coming out of the sea. He had ten horns and seven heads, with 10 crowns on his horns" (Revelation 13:1). This suggests a different form of government.

Clue 5: This lamblike beast has worldwide influence. It causes those who dwell on the earth to worship "the first beast" power (verse 12).

The United States didn't fit that picture a century or more ago. Like a lamb with its little horns, it seemed to have little power or authority. But now its global influence affects people everywhere financially, politically, and culturally.

The United States established a new type of government—democracy—with freedom of religion.

So let's review the five clues about the second beast, the lamblike nation of Revelation 13. We know that it would arise around 1798. It would be a new nation that would not be opposed to God, and would have no crowned head or kinglike authority. And it would rise to a position of worldwide influence.

John the revelator has pinpointed the rise of the United States of America precisely.

The nation that rose to champion religious and civil liberty will be a major player in the final end-time drama. But what exactly will that role be? Let's look at the evidence in Revelation 13:11: "Then I saw another beast, coming out of the earth. He had two horns like a lamb, but he spoke like a dragon." I'm afraid that the picture becomes grim rather quickly. The beast that had two horns like a lamb begins to speak "like a dragon."

WHAT HAPPENS TO THE NATION?

Obviously something happens to this nation. It started out lamblike, but eventually it will have a dragonlike roar. How do nations speak? They speak through their legislative bodies. The officials of nations speak for that nation as they enact laws. Revelation 13 describes the change from a lamblike beast to that of one sounding like a dragon, suggesting that it

Photodisc

will begin to use its growing power in a coercive manner. The picture gets darker as we read verse 12: "He exercised all the authority of the first beast on his behalf, and made the earth and its inhabitants worship the first beast, whose fatal wound had been healed."

Note carefully what this is saying. The second beast (nation) actually causes the inhabitants of earth to worship the first beast. That is, it will persuade people to adopt the fundamental principle of the medieval church—the fusion of church and state. Once again, aspects of society that have been kept apart will unite to enforce religious practices. The strong arm of the state will again coerce in a way similar to religious practices through the centuries. Once-Protestant America will join hands with religious oppression in a dangerous alliance of church and state.

ALL FORMS OF THE MEDIEVAL CHURCH UNITED CHURCH AND STATE.

You may wonder How could something like that ever happen? It seems impossible.

But wait, there's more. Look at Revelation 13:13, 14. Speaking of the second lamblike beast, John says: "He performed great and miraculous signs, even causing fire to come down from heaven to earth in full view of men. Because of the signs he was given power to do on behalf of the first beast, he deceived the inhabitants of the earth."

How can a country such as the United States give its allegiance to the beast of Revelation 13? Because of the miracles and wonders that soon will take place.

Many people assume that any miracle is God's doing, that it confirms someone's claims to truth. And God indeed performs signs and wonders as He thinks best. Sometimes miracles accompany the work of God, as in the case of Elijah on Mount Carmel. The fire that comes down from heaven is an allusion to the story in 1 Kings 18. But Satan too can work miracles. He can perform counterfeit signs and wonders. He can even bring miraculous-seeming fire.

As we saw before, Jesus warned His followers about what would hap-

pen during the last days: "For false Christs and false prophets will appear and perform great signs and miracles to deceive even the elect—if that were possible" (Matthew 24:24).

Spectacular signs and wonders are not necessarily a sign of divine favor. They can be an effort of our archenemy to deceive. And people who would rather have a sensational sign than the simple, straightforward truth of God's Word are setting themselves up for a fall. They will find themselves deceived by the spectacular works of a sinister power.

John reminds us: "They are spirits of demons performing miraculous signs, and they go out to the kings of the whole world, to gather them for the battle on the great day of God Almighty" (Revelation 16:14).

Even the greatest individuals, including politicians and national leaders, will unwittingly accept the wonder-working power of the great deceiver. That power enables the lamblike beast to cause all to worship the first beast. That's what will enable the United States to enforce religious intolerance.

A FALSE RELIGIOUS REVIVAL

Does it sound hard to believe? Think about what would happen if a religious revival swept across a country, one featuring great miracles or other wonders. Consider how easy it would be to rally around what appears to be the work of God, perhaps the last chance to save the nation from moral ruin—especially if a national crisis occurs at the same time.

As miracles happen, a spirit of unity prevails. People want to push the revival as far as it can go. They look for something that can unite everyone, some symbol of common worship. Why not emphasize the worship day itself? After all, it's something that most Christians share. At first glance the proposal seems so logical. Each Sunday the nation would all unite and worship in a spirit of unity. Wouldn't that bring a troubled country together and make it truly one nation under God?

> ELIJAH USED FIRE ON MOUNT CARMEL TO PROVE WHO WAS THE TRUE GOD, BUT SATAN WILL USE COUNTERFEIT FIRE TO TRY TO SUPPORT HIS END-TIME DECEPTIONS.

Does this sound far-fetched? Some religious leaders already have boldly suggested that a common day

PHOTODISC

of worship may be a partial solution to America's recurring energy crisis. By forbidding all driving on Sunday, except to church, the United States could save up to 15 percent of its gasoline supply.

Back in the 1970s Harold Lindsell proposed that for the purpose of conserving energy that "all businesses, including gasoline stations and restaurants, should close every Sunday" (*Christianity Today*, May 7, 1976). Lindsell expressed his conviction that such a move would satisfy both natural laws and the "will of God for all men." Sensing that it was highly unlikely that Sunday would voluntarily become a day of rest, he further suggested that one way to accomplish this would be "by force of legislative fiat through the duly elected officials of the people."

Some time ago the U.S. Supreme Court (*McGowan et al. v. Maryland*) ruled that in some instances Sunday laws may be enforced, not on the basis of religious considerations, but in the interests of safeguarding the health and welfare of the American people. The late Justice William O. Douglas disagreed and stated the following in his dissenting opinion to the majority decision of the court: "It seems to me plain that by these laws, the states compel one, under sanction of law, to refrain from work or recreation on Sunday because of the ma-

THE SUPREME COURT HAS RULED THAT SUNDAY LAWS MAY BE ENFORCED FOR NONRELIGIOUS REASONS.

jority's religious views on that day. The state by law makes Sunday a symbol of respect or adherence."

Are you aware that in the United States of America, right now, many are seeking to redefine religious liberty? U.S. Supreme Court Justice William H. Rehnquist wrote in 1985 *(Wallace v. Jaffree)* that "the 'wall of separation between church and state' is a metaphor based on bad history. . . . It should be frankly and explicitly abandoned." A vocal element of American society is reevaluating the entire issue of the wall of separation between church and state. The St. Louis *Post-Dispatch*, October 29, 1991, made an interesting observation: "As the second century of the Bill of Rights draws to a close, the Supreme Court is redefining what religious liberty will mean in the third century. Broadly, the court's new approach helps conventional religions while hurting unconventional ones."

The editorial proposes that the court is moving in the direction of stating what an acceptable religion is. And if you happen to fall into that conventional religion you can have the stamp of approval.

Events are moving us toward that day when the lamblike beast will roar like a dragon. Let's look at one more characteristic of this second beast: "He deceived the inhabitants of the earth. He ordered them to set up an image in honor of the beast who was wounded by the sword and yet lived. He was given power to give breath to the image of the first beast, so that it could speak and cause all who refused to worship the image to be killed" (Revelation 13:14, 15).

What does the phrase "set up an image in honor of the beast" mean?

An image of anything is something that looks like or resembles in some way something else. If a little boy is his dad's "spittin' image," he has many characteristics in common with his father.

Remember, we're dealing with symbols in Revelation. Thus the image of this beast won't be some literal object, that is, a statue or an idol. Rather it will be a repeat performance of what the beast did before—the religious intolerance and oppression that happened during the Dark Ages.

RELIGIOUS WITH CIVIL POWER

PHOTODISC

At the height of its power the medieval church—both West and East—clothed itself with civil power. It had the authority to appoint civil officials, punish dissenters, confiscate goods, imprison people, and even execute them. It was a powerful union of church and state.

So what will be an image of the beast? It will be another union of church and state, another ecclesiastical establishment clothed with civil power seeking to enforce its religious claims.

Think about this scenario. Consider a nation ripped apart by crime and riddled with lawlessness. People anguish because moral principles seem to have gone out the window. Kids are mowing down other kids in the schools. Violence and obscenity and abuse intensify. Society seems unable to win the war on drugs, terrorism, or the many other problems that disturb it.

THE UNITED STATES BECAME AN EXAMPLE OF THE PRINCIPLES OF RELIGIOUS LIBERTY ESTABLISHED BY THOMAS JEFFERSON.

People even now are demanding solutions. And the most instinctive reaction is: "There ought to be a law." Well-meaning citizens will band together to pass laws to save the country. They will think that they can rescue the nation by enforcing morality. "We've got to make our nation Christian [or Orthodox or Islamic or Hindu or whatever] again," they will say. Although it's a good motive, it's a bad procedure. The temptation is to pass laws forcing people to do by civil power what religion has failed to do by persuasive teaching and preaching.

PHOTODISC

Think of how powerful this new approach will become when

TNS-13

legislative initiatives are endorsed by a religious revival backed by signs and wonders.

In the United States Robert Grant, head of the Christian Voice organization, has said: "If Christians unite, we can do anything. We can pass any law or any amendment. And that's exactly what we intend to do." Another leader, Pat Robertson, wrote: "The next obligation that a citizen of God's world order owes is to himself. 'Remember the Sabbath day to keep it holy' is a command for the personal benefit of each citizen. . . . Higher civilizations rise when people can rest, think and draw inspiration from God. Laws in America that mandate a day of rest (Sunday laws) have been nullified as a violation of the separation of church and state. . . . As an outright insult to God and His plan, only those policies that can be shown to have a clearly secular purpose are recognized" (*The New World Order*, p. 236).

ALTHOUGH THE UNITED STATES HAS BECOME A SUPERPOWER, IT WILL NOT BE THE FINAL ONE.

Do you see his reasoning? He is saying we have outlawed the Sunday laws. But if we're going to bring this whole nation back to God, we have to worship God together. Therefore, it is logical in a time when moral values are waning—in a time of crisis—to unite on a point held in common, which, among most of the Christian churches, is Sunay observance. And it will require great conviction to hold on to the biblical Sabbath.

No, the United States is not the final superpower. That is yet to come when the rock cut without hands smashes all human nations and sets up God's divine kingdom.

PHOTODISC

Let me tell you about a man named Milton Schustek. He lived in Czechoslovakia during the years of Soviet domination and great religious oppression. When the Communists took over his country, he wanted to be free to read his Bible and continue his work as a pastor. But the Communists had other ideas. They had determined to turn all ministers into laborers. Milton knew that they wanted to send him as far away from his congregation as possible—far away to the coal mines.

But then he got an idea, one that might allow him to stay close to his pastoral work in the city of Prague. He thought of a job that nobody wanted—cleaning out the sewers. Nobody wanted to climb into those narrow, filthy culverts and clean them, hundreds of feet under the city.

Milton decided to see the Communist officials about taking that job. But first he got down on his knees and prayed. "Jesus," he said, "I want to worship You every Sabbath. Please help me to keep Your law and to be honest and faithful to You."

After being ushered in to see the local party official, Milton said to her, "I understand you want to ship me to the mines to work. Let me tell you something. My grandfather worked in the mines, and my father worked in the mines, and I'm willing to work in whatever mine you send me to. But I have a suggestion. You need someone to do the worst job you have—climbing down into those sewers. And I'm willing to do it. Why don't you assign me to clean the sewage system of Prague? I'd be happy to do it, because that would give me the privilege of worshipping my God here."

Something touched that Communist official's heart. She looked down at her desk, then glanced up at him and said, "Pastor, I'm not a godly woman. I'm just trying to fulfill work assignments. But I'll let you worship your God. Go and clean the sewer system."

I'll never forget the look on Milton's face as he related his story. He admitted it was a very tough, very dark, and very stressful job. But every day it was worth it, he said, because "I could worship my God in loyalty, in truth."

Someday each believer will be called upon to demonstrate that same kind of faith.

CHAPTER 14

LEAVE WHILE YOU STILL CAN!

Sometimes the lonely 83-year-old man cried himself to sleep. Five years earlier he'd been devastated when Eddie, his wife of 30 years, had died. Her calm and reserve balanced his feisty, sometimes cranky nature, and together they had traveled widely in their 1957 pink Cadillac with the gold-plated wheels.

Now the old man lived with his 16 cats and an 1883 player piano in a rustic lodge on the south shore of a lake near the base of a beautiful snowcapped mountain. He was a minor area celebrity—a fascinating front-porch storyteller who could keep tourists spellbound with his tales of the area.

But in the spring of 1980 state officials paid him a visit and warned him to leave immediately, because they feared the ancient volcanic mountain was about to erupt. But Harry Truman refused to leave his lodge at the base of Mount St. Helens. He'd been there for 54 years. "That mountain's part of Harry—and Harry's part of that mountain," he said. "I'm coming down feetfirst—or I'm not coming down at all." His defiant stand quickly spread to the national media, and Harry became an overnight celebrity.

On May 17 officials tried once more to reason with the old man of the mountain. Again he refused to leave. The next morning Mount St. Helens exploded with the force of a 23-megaton nuclear bomb. In seconds the top 1,300 feet of its nearly 10,000-foot peak blasted into the sky, burying Harry's lodge beneath hundreds of feet of volcanic ash and debris.

PHOTODISC

All through time people have heard the warning, "Leave now! Leave while you still can!" Nearly 2,000 years before Christ, God warned Lot and his family to flee the city of Sodom before its destruction along with the neighboring city of Gomorrah (Genesis 19).

The book of Revelation presents another urgent life-or-death message. Just as He had done almost 4,000 years ago with Sodom and Gomorrah, God is once again calling His followers out of another corrupt, wicked city. A city that so totally confuses those who stay in it that its very name has come to be considered a term for confusion: Babylon.

Now, right away, you may be thinking, *Well, I'm relieved, because I realize that I have nothing to worry about. Wherever this city of Babylon might be, I know for sure that I'm not in it.*

But I urge you to keep reading some astonishing facts from Scripture. It's possible you'll discover there is reason for you to be concerned.

Revelation 14:8 tells us: "A second angel followed and said, 'Fallen! Fallen is Babylon the Great, which made all the nations drink the maddening wine of her adulteries.'"

Ancient Babylon became a symbol in Scripture of everything that opposed God.

The angel mentioned here says that a great city named Babylon has fallen. Four chapters later, in Revelation 18:4, 5, we hear an urgent warning to leave it: "Then I heard another voice from heaven say: 'Come out of her, my people, so that you will not share in her sins, so that you will not receive any of her plagues; for her sins are piled up to heaven, and God has remembered her crimes.'"

It's clear from what we've just read that Babylon is a doomed city—and that God is calling His people to abandon it. "Leave town now!" He's saying. "Leave while you still can so that you don't share in the plagues that will punish sinful Babylon."

The ancient city of Babylon, rebuilt by King Nebuchadnezzar II, was erected on the site of the Tower of Babel. According to Genesis 10:10, it was here that Nimrod founded and ruled some of the earliest Mesopotamian cities, including Babylon.

Through the centuries Babylon the city extended its reach and its power to become an empire. Its fortunes rose and fell, and eventually the city and the empire came under the rule of King Nebuchadnezzar II—the one who proudly boasted, "Is not this the great Babylon I have built?" (Daniel 4:30).

After Nebuchadnezzar died, the empire of Babylon fell in the year 539 B.C. to the Medo-Persian Empire. Today what is left of ancient Babylon is located about an hour's drive south of Baghdad, Iraq. It's interesting that Iraq's infamous leader Saddam Hussein considered himself the reincarnation of Nebuchadnezzar. In fact, during his rule Saddam spent more than $500 million in an attempt to reconstruct the ancient city. He had more than 60 million bricks made to be placed in the city's walls, each engraved with the inscription "To King Nebuchadnezzar in the reign of Saddam Hussein."

Babylon's history is identified with false religion, with arrogance and pride, and with confusion. So when we find Babylon reappearing in the book of Revelation, we recognize it as symbolic of those very same characteristics. Only now, the ancient city of Babylon is mostly ruins—and the empire of Babylon is long gone.

WHAT IS BABYLON?

So what is this Babylon of Revelation? We've looked briefly at descriptions of Babylon in Revelation 14 and 18. In between, John, the author of Revelation, speaks in chapter 17 of an evil woman on a strange beast that has her allegiance to Babylon written on her forehead. "Then the angel carried me away in the Spirit into a desert," the prophet wrote. "There I saw a woman sitting on a scarlet beast that was covered with blasphemous names and had seven heads and ten horns. The woman was dressed in purple and scarlet, and was glittering with gold, precious stones and pearls. She held a golden cup in her hand, filled with abominable things and the filth of her adulteries. This title was written on her forehead: MYSTERY, BABYLON THE GREAT, THE MOTHER OF PROSTITUTES AND OF THE ABOMINATIONS OF THE EARTH" (Revelation 17:3-5).

The book of Revelation contains many prophetic symbols. One of them is that of a woman. And it's clear from a close study of the Bible that a woman in Scripture symbolizes a church (see Ephesians 5:23, 24; 2 Corinthians 11:2). Scripture also depicts the church as the bride of Christ. When she is faithful to her Lord, the Bible pictures her as a pure woman. But when she drifts away from her Lord into apostasy, the church commits spiritual adultery.

GOD DEPICTS SPIRITUAL UNFAITHFULNESS TO HIM THROUGH THE SYMBOL OF ADULTERY.

Fornication and adultery are terms the Bible uses to describe not only marital unfaithfulness between a husband and wife, but also unfaithfulness by God's people. Whenever the church leaves its true husband and lover, Jesus Christ, and takes up the practices of the world, it commits spiritual adultery. The apostle James makes it plain in these telling words: "You adulterous people, don't you know that friendship with the world is hatred toward God?" (James 4:4).

In contrast, Revelation 12 presents God's church as a pure woman. The church is His bride, and Christ is the husband. Christ, the head of the church, gives guidance and direction to His bride. The Bible pictures the true church as completely faithful to her husband—a woman who has not committed spiritual adultery.

The woman in Revelation 17:2 presents the opposite picture. She commits adultery with "the kings of the earth." Here we have a clear picture of false religion. The bejeweled woman passes around the wine of her

James Padgett

false doctrines, and the world becomes drunk. Now a harlot, she has left her true lover and is no longer the true church of Christ but the false church.

The Bible speaks about two great systems of reli-

Scripture portrays God's apostate people through the symbol of a fallen woman.

gion. One is centered on Jesus, who called Himself in John 14:6 "the way and the truth and the life." This church is based solidly on the teachings of Scripture. This is why Revelation 12 pictures the true church as a woman dressed in white. Her doctrines are pure—she is loyal to her true Master and has not compromised with error. Truth and error, as water and oil, cannot and do not mix.

THE TRUE CHURCH IS LOYAL TO HER MASTER AND IS NOT COMPROMISED WITH ERROR.

But as we have seen, in addition to the woman in white, the Bible describes a woman in purple and scarlet (the colors of kings, emperors, and other rulers) with a cup of wine—representing false doctrine—in her hand. She is the great apostate mother church, and many churches have drunk of her wine. The Bible says that she rides upon a scarlet-colored beast, and in the Bible, as we have already seen, an animal represents a political system.

This false church, decked in costly garments, has left her true lover, Jesus, by seeking political power and placing human traditions and the decrees of church councils above the Word of God. She is an adulteress in the sense that she has betrayed scriptural teachings and compromised her first loyalty to God by political alliances and entanglements. Scripture portrays her as the great mother church, and along with her are other churches that also have left true biblical doctrines.

Revelation's picture of a woman on a scarlet-colored beast represents a union of church and state. Yet here the emphasis is on the dominance of the church over the state powers—the woman is riding the animal. The Bible predicted that this false church, in passing around its wine cup, would lead multitudes to drink of its false doctrines and thus accept error in the place of truth.

To learn the identity of spiritual Babylon in the New Testament, we need to go back to literal

GOD PICTURES HIS FAITHFUL PEOPLE BY THE SYMBOL OF A PURE WOMAN DRESSED IN WHITE AND AS A BRIDE.

RUSSELL HARLAN

Babylon in the Old Testament. Scripture saw old Babylon as exemplifying certain characteristics that are also true of spiritual Babylon in the book of Revelation.

CHARACTERISTICS OF BABYLON

1. BABYLON: A SYSTEM BASED ON HUMAN POWER AND PERSPECTIVES RATHER THAN DIVINE TEACHINGS.

The first characteristic we see clearly in Nebuchadnezzar's boast, recorded in Daniel 4:30: "Is not this the great Babylon I have built as the royal residence, by my mighty power and for the glory of my majesty?" So one characteristic of Babylon is that it is a human-oriented system of religion, one that seeks power through human alliances and ways of doing things.

Nebuchadnezzar recorded his pride in rebuilding Babylon by an inscription stamped on the very bricks of the city.

Siegfried Horn Museum

The true church of God directs men and women to Jesus Christ as its only head. The false system points men and women to human religious leaders rather than to Jesus alone. Speaking of Jesus, Colossians 1:18 says: "And he is the head of the body, the church; he is the beginning and the firstborn from among the dead, so that in everything he might have the supremacy."

The true church of God leads men and women to Jesus, who alone can forgive their sins and release them from the bondage of evil. Revelation's spiritual Babylon is an earthly system of religion based primarily on human tradition, with a human leader. It redirects the focus from a divine Savior to human priests. The teachings of church prelates, ecclesiastical councils, and religious dogma replace the plain instruction of God's Word. Throughout history it has persecuted those who did not accept its claims (Revelation 17:6) and has swayed kings and political leaders down through the centuries (verse 2).

2. BABYLON: A SYSTEM OF RELIGION BASED ON THE FALSE TEACHING OF THE SOUL'S IMMORTALITY.

Another characteristic of ancient Babylon that applies to spiritual Babylon appears in Ezekiel 8:13, 14: "He said, 'You will see them doing things that are even more detestable.' Then he brought me to the entrance to the north gate of the house of the Lord, and I saw women sitting there, mourning for Tammuz."

Who was Tammuz, and why were the women weeping? Tammuz was the Babylonian god of vegetation. The Babylonians believed that when spring gave way to summer and the summer heat scorched the crops, Tammuz died. Therefore, they wept and prayed that he might return from the underworld. As with each pagan culture before them, the Babylonians accepted the falsehood of the immortal soul and the various kinds of afterlife associated with it. And the concept continually threatened to creep in even among God's people.

The whole Christian concept of the immortal soul did not come from the Bible. Instead, it slipped into the church through pagan sources, particularly as developed in Greek philosophy. Early Christian apologists used neo-Platonic concepts to reach the pagan world around them. William E. Gladstone (1809-1898), four-time prime minister of Great Britain who in his youth considered entering the ministry and throughout his life had a strong interest in theology, observed that "the doctrine of natural, as distinguished from Christian, immortality . . . crept

THE TRUE CHURCH OF GOD LEADS PEOPLE TO JESUS, WHO ALONE CAN FORGIVE THEIR SINS.

S. W. PRODUCTIONS

into the church, by a back door as it were" (*Studies Subsidiary to the Works of Bishop Butler*, 1896 edition, p. 195). The distinguished British statesman was right. In previous chapters we discovered that Scripture teaches that only God is immortal (1 Timothy 6:16). Immortality is a gift He gives us at His return (1 Thessalonians 4:16, 17).

Again, we have seen that the Bible is clear about what happens to people when they die. "For the wages of sin is death, but the gift of God is eternal life in Christ Jesus our Lord" (Romans 6:23). "His breath goeth forth, he returneth to his earth; in that very day his thoughts perish" (Psalm 146:4, KJV). "It is not the dead who praise the Lord, those who go down to silence" (Psalm 115:17). "The living know that they will die, but the dead know nothing" (Ecclesiastes 9:5).

THE CONCEPT OF THE IMMORTAL SOUL CAME FROM PAGAN SOURCES.

The Babylonians, as did most ancient people, believed that an immortal soul left the body at death and lived on. Most of Christianity continues this false teaching in its doctrine of the immortal soul. Any church that neglects, overlooks, or rejects the biblical teaching on the nonimmortality of the soul is drinking from the false doctrines of the wine cup of Babylon, whether they know it or not.

3. BABYLON: A FALSE SYSTEM OF RELIGION TINGED WITH SUN WORSHIP.

We come now to a third characteristic of Babylon that infiltrated even God's Old Testament people. "He then brought me into the inner court of the house of the Lord, and there at the entrance to the temple, between the portico and the altar, were about twenty-five men. With their backs toward the temple of the Lord and their faces toward the east, they were bowing down to the sun in the east" (Ezekiel 8:16).

The prophet Ezekiel saw the men following the widespread pagan practice of sun worship. Turning their faces toward the east, they knelt and worshipped the sun god as the sun rose in the sky. At the same time, they turned their back on the Temple, the place where the symbol of the God of Israel dwelled on earth. The Babylonians worshipped the sun god Shamash. God of justice and judge of all the other gods, Shamash appears carved in relief at the top of King Hammurabi's famous law code stela. The relief shows him presenting a scepter to Hammurabi.

It's interesting that not only the Egyptians and Babylonians, but also the Romans, worshipped the sun. Sir James G. Frazer observes that "among the Romans the worship of the sun was from immemorial antiquity" (*The Worship of Nature*, vol. 1, p. 529). Constantine, the pagan Roman emperor, worshiped the sun. One side of the coins he issued had his own picture while on the other side was that of the sun god—*Sol Invictus*, "the invincible Sun." Later, after he became a Christian, he minted coins with Christ represented on one side and the sun god on the opposite side! Arthur P. Stanley wrote: "His [Constantine's] coins bore on the one side the letters of the name of Christ; on the other, the figure of the sun god, as if he could not bear to relinquish the patronage of the bright luminary" (*Lectures on the History of the Eastern Church*, p. 184).

The practices of pagan sun worship continued to linger in the church. Even as late as the middle of the fifth century we find Pope Leo I rebuking worshippers at St. Peter's because they kept turning around and bowing toward the sun before entering the basilica.

Rites and imagery connected with sun worship thus slipped into the Christian church during its early centuries.

From time to time people say to me, "Mark, you talk and write about Jesus and His second coming, but you also mention the Bible Sabbath a great deal. Why?"

Now are you beginning to see why? The book of Revelation describes a church that would absorb and perpetuate the ancient pagan principles of Babylon. The entire world would sip the wine of its polluted

THE MESOPOTAMIAN SUN GOD, SHAMASH, HERE APPEARS AT THE TOP OF THE STELE OF HAMMURABI'S LAW CODE.

SIEGFRIED HORN MUSEUM

teachings. Unknowingly they'd continue ideas and practices that came down from Babylon and Egypt. Even the reforming Protestant churches would accept many of them.

Lewis Brown comments that "one cannot well refer to those cults of Babylon and Egypt and the rest as dead religions" (*The Believing World*, p. 112). Why? "For the echo of their ancient thunder is still to be heard reverberating in almost every form of faith existing today." Ancient image worship, sun worship, and belief in the immortality of the human soul still shape religious belief. Yes, the echo of that thunder is still heard in the church today.

During the early centuries of the church one of the things its leaders did was to substitute the pagan sun day for the Christian Sabbath. Catholic William L. Gildea wrote that "the sun was a foremost god with heathendom. . . . The sun has worshippers at this hour in Persia and other lands. . . . There is, in truth, something royal, kingly about the sun, making it a fit emblem of Jesus, the Sun of Justice. Hence the church in these countries would seem to have said, 'Keep that old pagan name [Sunday]. It shall remain consecrated, sanctified.' And thus the pagan Sunday, dedicated to Balder, became the Christian Sunday, sacred to Jesus" (*The Catholic World*, March 1894, p. 809).

RITES AND IMAGERY CONNECTED WITH SUN WORSHIP SLIPPED INTO THE EARLY CHURCH.

Arthur P. Stanley observed that "the retention of the old pagan name of Dies Solis, for Sunday, is, in a great measure, owing to the union of pagan and Christian sentiment with which the first day of the week was recommended by Constantine to his subjects—pagan and Christian alike—as the 'venerable' day of the sun" (*Lectures on the History of the Eastern Church*, p. 184).

Dr. Edward Hiscox, author of *The Baptist Manual*, speaking to the Baptist convention, said: "What a pity that it [Sunday] comes branded with the mark of paganism, and christened with the name of a sun god, when adopted and sanctioned by the papal apostasy, and bequeathed as a sacred legacy to Protestants."

God's people will search for a church with pure teachings.

S. W. Productions

Sunday has slipped into the Christian church not based on a command of God, but through pagan sources. Surprisingly, most Protestant churches have not protested enough. They have accepted a counterfeit day "bequeathed as a sacred legacy from Rome."

On page 99 of a book called *The Question Box*, Catholic author F. G. Lentz confirms this, as he writes: "In keeping Sunday, non-Catholics are simply following the practice of the Catholic Church for 1800 years, a tradition, and not a Bible ordinance."

Also, most churches teach the doctrine that the soul is immortal, and thus unwittingly worship at the shrine of pagan belief and philosophy. Most ancient peoples believed that the spirits of the dead could come back. If you believe that the soul is immortal, who is to say it cannot communicate with the living? Your mind would then be open for great deceptions in the end-time.

The book of Revelation leads us away from Babylonian errors to God's truth in His Word. I don't want to accept errors that began in Babylon, then spread to pagan Rome and the early church, and I'm sure you don't want to either. The symbol of the harlot applies to every church that openly rebels against the commandments of God. False Christendom—based on human tradition and divided into hundreds of denominations—is truly a Babylon of confusion.

Today the religious world is largely confused—confused on the state of human beings in death, confused on the Sabbath question, confused

REVELATION 17'S IDENTIFYING CHARACTERISTICS OF SPIRITUAL BABYLON		
1	the great harlot (verses 1, 2)	an apostate religious system (James 4:4; Hosea 2:13)
2	the kings of the earth (verse 2)	political leaders
3	committed fornication (verse 2)	an illicit union; the bride of Christ is united to her true lover, Jesus Christ, while Babylon, the great harlot, demands support from political powers (2 Corinthians 11:2)
4	inhabitants of the earth (verse 2)	the people or citizenry
5	drunk with wine	intoxicated with false doctrine
6	woman sitting on scarlet-colored beast (verse 3)	fallen church directing state activities
7	golden cup (verse 4)	since this cup contains the wine of Babylon, it overflows with false doctrine
8	Mystery, Babylon the Great, Mother of Harlots (verse 55)	the great mother church
9	the woman church with the blood of the saints (verse 6)	a persecuting church

about whether the head of the church is God in heaven or a human being on earth.

Perhaps you find yourself wrestling with some of the issues raised in this chapter. You believe the Bible Sabbath to be true or that when people die they sleep until resurrection morning. Perhaps you wonder if somehow you might have one foot in your church and the other in God's true church.

God summons the members of His invisible, true church, if they would be safe, to come out of fallen Babylon. Soon time will run out. All human beings will have to make their final choice—for Christ or for tradition, for truth or for error, for the Scriptures or for human substitutes.

This could be your moment to decide. Will you not tell Jesus, "Lord, I hear Your call—'Fallen! Fallen is Babylon the Great!' . . . 'Come out of her, my people' "?

CHAPTER 15

FINAL SHOWDOWN

In August of 1945 atomic bombs fell on Hiroshima and Nagasaki, Japan, leading to the swift surrender of that nation to the Allied powers and bringing an end to World War II. Shortly after that, in an early September 2 public speech General Douglas MacArthur expressed his sense of foreboding for the future. "We have had our last chance," he said. "If we do not devise some greater and more equitable system, Armageddon will be at our door."

During the cold war that followed World War II, commentators often described the specter of a worldwide nuclear holocaust as a looming Armageddon. And today the term *Armageddon* in popular thought has come to be synonymous with a final, catastrophic battle or calamity that could end all life on earth.

Armageddon will indeed be the last battle ever fought on earth, and both the word and the battle it names come straight from the book of Revelation.

Some time ago I read an interesting story that clearly illustrates what some people believe about the return of our Lord. Linda, a young mother, was driving home from shopping when a meteor suddenly streaked across the night sky. Unaccustomed to such a starry display, she anxiously pressed down on the accelerator.

"All I wanted to do was to get home and be with my son," she later said. "I was sure that Jesus was coming that very minute!"

PHOTODISC

EVEN AFTER VICTORY IN WORLD WAR II, GENERAL DOUGLAS MACARTHUR WORRIED THAT ARMAGEDDON WOULD COME, UNLESS THE WORLD CHANGED.

It's true that the Bible teaches that Jesus will return soon to Planet Earth. But it also makes clear that specific events must take place before His arrival. A significant part of being ready for His coming involves understanding the biblical teaching about what will occur during earth's last days.

This sequence of events—this preview of earth's final headlines—begins in Revelation 14:9, 10: "If anyone worships the beast and his image and receives his mark on the forehead or on the hand, he, too, will drink of the wine of God's fury, which has been poured full strength into the cup of his wrath. He will be tormented with burning sulfur in the presence of the holy angels and of the Lamb."

Before Jesus returns, the mark of the beast will be enforced upon men and women throughout this world. We read in Revelation 13:17 that all classes of people—rich and poor, small and great, free and slave—will come under pressure to accept the "mark . . . or the number of his name."

Only those with the mark will have permission to buy and sell. Those who do not have it, the Bible reveals, become the objects of an economic and social boycott. Ultimately they will face the threat of death.

S. W. Productions

A QUESTION OF LOYALTY

The final issue of the long conflict between Christ and Satan—between good and evil—will focus on the question of loyalty. God has always examined people to see if they love Him enough to remain loyal to Him. In Eden the test of loyalty was a tree in the middle of the garden. For the prophet Daniel's three friends the issue involved the second commandment, which forbade the worship of graven images. Since the three Hebrews would not bow down to the image and violate the second commandment, the Babylonian authorities tried to execute them.

Scripture reveals God's test of loyalty.

And in the last generation God's test of loyalty will focus on the fourth commandment. After the enforcement of the mark of the beast, humanity will have divided into two classes—those who receive the mark of the beast and those who receive the seal of God. That is, those who are disloyal and those who are loyal to God. Each person alive will be on one side or the other. And after each person has made that final, irrevocable decision, Revelation 14:10 says that God's wrath, unmingled with mercy, will be "poured full strength into the cup of his wrath."

Until then the Lord has ur-

PHOTODISC

gently appealed to the people of earth, warning them of the tragic consequences of choosing to ignore His mercy. But many will reject that mercy, and then they will learn to their great sorrow the tragic and fearful consequences of their decision.

We find in Revelation 15 and 16 that God's wrath in earth's last hour will come in the form of the seven last plagues, reserved for those who receive the mark of the beast. Those who yield to human traditions and human laws, selling out their devotion to Christ, will ultimately experience the unmitigated wrath of God.

The "wine of the wrath of God" is a strange expression for a God of love. What exactly is it? Disappointed, heartbroken, sorrowful about their choices, yes—but God is not hostile toward sinners. "The wine of the wrath of God," is another expression for His judgments upon sin. He allows all to make eternal choices. The logical result of sinful, rebellious decisions is separation from God, who is the source of life. If He permitted sin to go on forever, rebellion just might engulf the entire universe. The judgments of God—the seven last plagues—is what will happen to the unsaved because of their own choices.

"THE WINE OF THE WRATH OF GOD" IS ANOTHER EXPRESSION FOR GOD'S JUDGMENTS UPON SIN.

But what happens to God's people during this time of calamity unlike any other crisis in human history? God's Word assures us that His children will not only remain alive during this time but will be protected by His grace. While the plagues fall all around them, the saved will be protected. God's people will go through this great tribulation and emerge triumphant. At the end of the plagues Christ will deliver His people and take them home.

Thus, as we discovered in earlier chapters, Scripture does not support the popular teaching of the secret rapture. Revelation 15:8 tells us that "no one could enter the [heavenly] temple until the seven plagues of the seven angels were completed." If God were to rapture or take His people to heaven before He poured out the plagues, they would obviously have entered the heavenly temple. But the Bible clearly says that nobody can enter the temple in heaven until the seven last plagues are over with.

SEVEN LAST PLAGUES

Before the seven last plagues begin, God's angel will have made a solemn announcement: "Let him who does wrong continue to do wrong; let him who is vile continue to be vile; let him who does right continue to do right; and let him who is holy continue to be holy" (Revelation 22:11). God's judgment will have decided every case, for either eternal life or eternal death. The door of God's mercy will have shut, ushering in the "time of trouble" spoken of by the prophet Daniel in Daniel 12:1 (KJV).

The most vivid description of this period of earth's history cannot begin to approach its reality as the wicked drink the cup of God's wrath unmixed with mercy. John received a preview of this terrible time of trouble that would take place just before the return of Jesus and the deliverance of His people. "Then I heard a loud voice from the temple saying to the seven angels, 'Go, pour out the seven bowls of God's wrath on the earth' " (Revelation 16:1).

John's description of the plagues echoes those that fell upon Egypt. The first plague to strike the wicked is "ugly and painful sores" (verse 2), possibly resembling the boils suffered by the Egyptians during their seventh plague. Can you imagine the impact such an affliction will have? Schools will close and factories will have to shut down. Stores will not be able to open. Hospitals and walk-in clinics will overflow with people seeking emergency treatment, but the doctors and nurses will be suffering from the same problem.

Notice specifically upon whom the first plague falls—those who receive the mark of the beast. Why were they willing to accept the mark? They wanted physical security. The antichrist power, uniting with polit-

THE SEVEN LAST PLAGUES
REVELATION 16:2-21

1. Painful sores.
2. Sea as blood.
3. Fresh water as blood.
4. Sun scorches the unsaved.
5. Darkness on the seat of the beast.
6. Armageddon—earth's last war.
7. Earthquakes and hailstones devastate earth.

JESUS RETURNS

ical authorities, declared that unless each individual received the mark of the beast they would be fired, imprisoned, beaten, tortured, unable to buy or sell. Eventually they would face death.

The first plague shows the folly of trusting your physical security to anyone except Jesus. The recipients of the mark of the beast sell out their souls for a promise of physical security. But in return they receive the very thing they sought to avoid: physical affliction—in this case, sores covering their bodies. The first plague declares that there is absolutely no physical security outside of Christ.

Then while people are still in agony, another calamity strikes. "The second angel poured out his bowl on the sea, and it turned into blood like that of a dead man, and every living thing in the sea died" (verse 3). What a sight—and what a stench—as the creatures of the sea wash ashore. People will stumble over one another as they flee from the beaches.

"THE SECOND ANGEL POURED OUT HIS BOWL ON THE SEA, . . . AND EVERY LIVING THING IN THE SEA DIED."

PHOTODISC

The third plague, brought to view in verse 4, is closely associated with the second: "The third angel poured out his bowl on the rivers and springs of water, and they became blood." A person turns on the faucet to get a drink—and instead of water, blood flows! Could anything be worse? Why does God allow this ghastly plague? Why do the unsaved receive blood to drink? "For they have shed the blood of your saints and prophets, and you have given them blood to drink as they deserve" (verse 6).

The beastlike church-and-state union commands allegiance. Anyone who doesn't worship the beast faces the death penalty. In the third plague God reveals that all life comes from Him. Blood is a symbol of life. Remember Moses' statement in Leviticus 17:11: "For the life of a creature is in the blood." When Jesus shed His blood on Calvary's cross, He revealed His amazing love for us before the universe. He redeemed us from the condemnation of sin. We are His by creation and redemption. Our lives are Christ's.

PHOTODISC

At this time when the wicked are perishing of thirst and have nothing to drink but blood, the promise of Isaiah 33:16 becomes real to those who walk righteously: "His bread will be supplied, and his water will not fail him." While this promise may sound like poetry now, then it will be worth more than the wealth of all the world's banks.

Because the wicked shed the blood of the righteous, God punishes them with plagues of blood.

Next the fourth angel pours out his bowl, scorching unsaved humanity with fire and great heat (Revelation 16:8, 9). We can only imagine the effect of this heat on blood-clogged waterways. Those who receive the mark of the beast have unwittingly accepted pagan sun worship by knowingly honoring a counterfeit day of worship. The fourth plague alludes to true worship only in Christ.

The fifth angel follows, spreading darkness throughout the land, while unsaved humanity continues to suffer from the earlier plagues, gnawing their tongues in pain (verses 10, 11). This text indicates that the plagues are not all universal or immediately fatal, since those under the fifth plague still suffer from the sores of the first plague. They have looked to the beast for light, but now wander in darkness. Jesus is "the light of the world" (John 8:12). His Word is a "lamp to [our] feet and a light for [our] path" (Psalm 119:105). The fifth plague shouts in trumpet tones that all light and truth is only in Jesus. The darkness of error engulfs the antichrist and all of his followers.

Apparently the plagues fall successively instead of simultaneously, as their effects overlap. The accumulation of suffering becomes unspeakable! Then comes the sixth plague, ushering in the great battle of Armageddon.

Revelation 16:13 describes "three evil spirits that looked like frogs; they came out of the mouth of the dragon, out of the mouth of the beast and out of the mouth of the false prophet." These unclean spirits, symbolizing the "spirits of demons" (verse 14), will "go out to the kings of the whole world, to gather them for the battle on the great day of God Almighty" (verse 14).

The battle of Armageddon focuses on the final offensive of the combined forces of rebel religious powers as they mobilize against God's people. They seek to destroy completely those loyal to God. All living at that time will be involved—on one side or the other—in the final conflict.

THE LAST BATTLE

In the final moment of time, when it looks as if God's people face annihilation, the last phase of the battle occurs. Christ, the King of the east, returns from the sky, accompanied by His armies from the sky. The artillery from heaven slay the wicked. This is Armageddon! The sixth and seventh plagues assure us that victory over the forces of evil is in God's hands.

"The seventh angel poured out his bowl into the air, and out of the temple came a loud voice from the throne, saying, 'It is done!' Then there came flashes of lightning, rumblings, peals of thunder and a severe earthquake. No earthquake like it has ever occurred since man has been on earth, so tremendous was the quake. . . . Every island fled away and the mountains could not be found" (verses 17-20).

This catastrophic convulsion of the earth levels the cities as well as

Arlo Greer

ARLO GREER

the mountains. Next come "huge hailstones of about a hundred pounds each" (verse 21). The devastation from such a hailstorm is beyond comprehension. But the Bible tells us that the Lord Himself will interrupt the conflict as He rides forth with the armies of heaven to deliver His people.

We can learn a lesson for the future from the past. After the children of Israel had endured centuries of slavery in Egypt, the time arrived for God to fulfill His promise to deliver them from bondage. He sent Moses and Aaron to Pharaoh with the message "Let my people go" (Exodus 5:1). Note verse 2: "Who is the Lord, that I should obey him?" And the ruler's haughty response ignited God's wrath.

Through the 10 plagues that fell on Egypt just before God delivered His people, the Lord answered Pharaoh's question in a dramatic way. The final chilling plague resulted in the death of all the firstborn in Egypt, beginning with the pharaoh's family. With an aching heart, the Egyptian ruler learned to take the warnings of God seriously.

But what was happening to the children of Israel during this time of great suffering and turmoil throughout the land? While Moses and Aaron had requested Pharaoh to deliver God's people from bondage, they had also instructed their fellow

HAIL AND OTHER PLAGUES WILL STRIKE THE EARTH AS THE WICKED CONTINUE TO REBEL AGAINST GOD.

PHOTODISC

FINAL EVENTS

OUR DAY	THE TEST	CLOSE OF PROBATION	DELIVERANCE
Signs of Christ's Return	**Mark of the Beast v. Seal of God**	**Seven Plagues Poured Out**	**Jesus Returns**
False Christs, famines, pestilences, earthquakes, wars, international conflicts, peace movements, moral breakdown, lawlessness, gospel to the world.	A time of final decision for all humanity. God's people persecuted and imprisoned. Economic boycott. Death decree.	God's people protected. Wicked afflicted by the plagues.	Righteous dead resurrected. Righteous living translated. Wicked destroyed by glory of Jesus' return.

Israelites how to respond to the Lord's remarkable intervention.

On the fourteenth day of the first month of the ancient Israelite year they were to slaughter a lamb and sprinkle its blood on the doorposts of their houses. Such a sign was not done lightly. It clearly showed a difference between those willing to trust the God of Israel and those who were either hesitant or afraid to declare themselves, fearing reprisals by the Egyptians. It was a night of testing for Israel as well as for the pharaoh.

Just as God had warned, at midnight the destroying angel passed through the land, visiting death upon the homes of all those without God's identifying mark—the blood on the doorpost—and sparing those families who had visibly declared their loyalty to Him regardless of the consequences. That night the children of Israel left for the Promised Land under God's protection.

It will be just the same in earth's last hours. The final plagues will fall on those who have rejected or neglected God's deliverance and salvation. But those who have chosen the blood of the Lamb for forgiveness and cleansing from their sins will be delivered.

By our lives we are deciding today which side we will be on—God's side or that of a rebel angel. When the plagues begin to fall, it will be too late to change allegiance. Opportunity's door will have already closed forever.

PHOTODISC

GOD PROMISES THAT HE WILL SHELTER US AS A CHICK UNDER HIS WINGS.

A story tells of an Australian lumberjack who built a simple cabin at the edge of a forest. One day as he returned home from work, he was stunned and heartbroken to find his home reduced to a heap of smoldering ruins. All that remained were a few pieces of charred lumber and some blackened metal. Walking out to where his old chicken coop had stood, the man discovered only a mound of ashes and some charred wire. Aimlessly he shuffled through the debris. Then glancing down at his feet, his eye caught a curious sight—a mound of blackened feathers. Idly he kicked it over. Four fuzzy baby chicks scrambled out, miraculously protected by the body of their loving mother.

In some of the most beautiful and meaningful language of Scripture, God in Psalm 91:4 describes what He longs to do for every one of His children on earth when the plagues fall. "He will cover you with his feathers, and under his wings you will find refuge."

GOD'S ASSURANCE TO HIS FOLLOWERS

God has given wonderful assurance to those who choose to follow Him. Down through the ages Christians have memorized the words of Psalm 91, taking courage in the promise set forth in verses 7 and 10: "A thousand may fall at your side, ten thousand at your right hand, but it will not come near you." "No harm will befall you." The good news of the Bible is that while the plagues will be falling all around those loyal to God, He will give His angels charge over them (verse 11).

We already know how the battle of Armageddon will turn out—know who will walk away, shaken perhaps, but with a song on their lips. In Revelation 15:3 John names that song as "the song of Moses the servant of God and the song of the Lamb."

The valiant heroes of earth's final conflict—those qualified to sing this victory song—are those "who obey God's commandments and remain faithful to Jesus" (Revelation 14:12). What a group to belong to!

Soon the sun will rise on the last-ever morning on the earth—a golden morning when all battles are over forever, when we will be reunited with those we've lost in death, and when Jesus returns in unspeakable glory to take His people home.

CHAPTER 16

A THOUSAND YEARS OF GUARANTEED PEACE

The time was the Roaring Twenties, and a young woman from New York City named Rose did her level best to live up to the times. High-spirited and talented, she attended many parties and shows and enjoyed the attentions of admiring young men. She loved to fly, and traveled across the United States by air several times, quite an unusual adventure in those early days of the airplane.

But suddenly, at the age of 21, an epidemic of a condition called sleeping sickness struck her down. The disease began with a series of nightmares that proved prophetic. Rose dreamed that she was imprisoned in an inaccessible castle—one shaped like herself. She'd become a statue and had fallen into a sleep so deep that nothing could awaken her. The world had come to a stop.

Then Rose awoke immobile, frozen in an awkward position on the bed. Her doctor said it was just catatonia, which would go away in a week. But that inaccessible castle did not dissolve as the months and years passed. Rose remained trapped in some incomprehensible state, looking as if she were trying her hardest to remember something. Eventually her body became rigid, and she had to be committed to an institution, where she lay in a bed—her face completely expressionless as the decades passed.

Then, in June of 1969, Dr. Oliver Sacks began administering a newly developed drug to the few survivors of the sleeping sickness. L-dopa was designed to counter a dopamine insufficiency detected in the

PHOTODISC

brains of those who had died from Parkinson's disease, a condition thought to be related to Rose's problem.

Dr. Sacks injected her with 1.5 grams of L-dopa, and the woman awakened from her long sleep. During the following days her eyes brightened up and she lost her rigidity. Beginning to feel sudden bursts of energy and excitement, she asked for the use of a tape recorder and began composing songs and light verse—all reminiscent of the 1920s. She was full of anecdotes about people she thought of as current public figures—again all from the twenties. For her, she was still living in the era of her youth.

THE SURVIVORS OF THE SLEEPING SICKNESS EPIDEMIC WERE STILL TRAPPED IN THE MEMORIES OF LONG AGO.

PHOTODISC

But one day the truth began to dawn on her. Looking anxious and bewildered, she told Dr. Sacks, "Things can't last. Something awful is coming. God knows what it is, but it's bad as they come." Thereafter the old symptoms began to reappear again. And slowly Rose sank back into her trance. The almost half-century gap was simply too great for her to bridge. Rose still felt like that 20-year-old girl who had always been the life of the party. She could not fathom who the 64-year-old woman staring back at her in the mirror was. As Dr. Sacks wrote: "She is a Sleeping Beauty whose 'awakening' was unbearable and who will never be awakened again."

It is hard for us, of course, to imagine the kind of shattering experience that such an awakening creates—what it must be like to wake up suddenly in a strange new world, to have lost yourself somewhere far back in time. But I believe that each one of us is going to experience something even more startling than what Rose went through. We are going to find ourselves suddenly thrust into a whole new world that none of us could begin to imagine.

A FINAL AWAKENING

Paul tells us about this climactic event: "For the Lord himself will come down from heaven, with a loud command, with the voice of the archangel and with the trumpet call of God, and the dead in Christ will rise first. After that, we who are still alive and are left will be caught up together with them in the clouds to meet the Lord in the air. And so we will be with the Lord forever" (1 Thessalonians 4:16, 17).

The second coming of Christ will arrive on our planet like a star bursting in the heavens. The Bible tells us that every human eye will see Jesus Christ when He appears in glory (Revelation 1:7), and every human being, both the living and the resurrected redeemed, will suddenly find themselves confronted with the kingdom of God. In the brilliant light of Christ's return the history of this planet will seem dark indeed, marred as it has been with cruelty and tragedy. At that moment we will feel, as never before, the loss, the waste, the suffering of our centuries of separation from God.

Christ's second advent will bring the saved new dawning, a new life. Those awakening from the graves will feel as if time had stood still since the day they closed their eyes in death. Now they're suddenly alive—and more alive than they've ever been before.

But the sad fact is that for some people, their awakening won't be wonderful news. The new day of God's kingdom will seem strange and terrifying. And what many people don't realize is that these two different awakenings—these two different fates—happen as two different events. Scripture presents *two* general resurrections—the resurrection to life and the resurrection to damnation. Jesus said: "Do not be amazed at this, for

Clyde Provonsha

The Bible tells us that every human eye will see Jesus when He appears in glory.

a time is coming when all who are in their graves will hear his voice and come out—those who have done good will rise to live, and those who have done evil will rise to be condemned" (John 5:28, 29).

Notice carefully: every human being will be resurrected or awakened from sleep at one of the two resurrections. Jesus' words are clear. "All who are in their graves will hear his voice." Then our Lord describes the two resurrections: (1) the resurrection to life and (2) the resurrection to condemnation. "Blessed and holy are those who have part in the first resurrection," Revelation 20:6 tells us.

By identifying this as the *first* resurrection, God lets us know that a second one will also occur. And by specifying that those raised in the first resurrection are the faithful dead—the blessed and holy—we also learn that the rest of the dead, the unfaithful, will come up from the grave at some other time.

What happens to those who rise in the *first* resurrection? "The second death has no power over them, but they will be priests of God and of

Christ and will reign with him for a thousand years" (verse 6). So in this first resurrection—the resurrection to life—the dead in Christ are caught up to meet Jesus in the sky. They will journey to heaven and reign with him for 1,000 years. The resurrection of damnation takes place later.

What about believers who are alive when Christ comes? The Bible tells us that when Jesus returns, the dead in Christ are resurrected first and meet Him in the sky. Changed and transformed, the living righteous also rise up to join Christ and the resurrected dead (1 Thessalonians 4:16, 17). Paul gives us a wonderful assurance: "We will all be changed. . . . For the perishable must clothe itself with the imperishable, and the mortal with immortality" (1 Corinthians 15:51-53).

The word "mortal" means subject to death—capable of dying. Our mortal bodies get tired, get sick, and get old. But when we look up and see Jesus coming, new life will pulsate through our bodies with incredible energy and vitality. We will ascend into the air toward a glorious destiny with our Redeemer.

THE FATE OF THE WICKED

But what about the wicked? What about those who rejected God's love?

Revelation 6:15-17 describes them as praying for the rocks to fall on them. Instead of seeing a Savior, they see the face of a disappointed Father, grieving over the fate of rebellious children. That's what fear and guilt and rebellion do to people. To them the Lamb of God resembles a raging lion. Although they are people God wanted to save—people for whom Christ died—they just didn't respond to His appeals. They refused to be rescued, because they rejected the message of salvation.

Tragically enough, many people find the good news of salvation not to be good news at all. Paul writes: "For the message of the cross is foolishness to those who are perishing, but to us who are being saved it is the power of God" (1 Corinthians 1:18).

It's the same message but received very differently, depending on a person's response to God's appeals. To some it's just a foolish old myth that fails to awaken their interest. Others accept it as the power of God—

PHOTODISC

and it becomes just that! It's not that God gives good news to some and bad news to others. No, He presents grace to every human being, just as His sunshine and rain blesses both the just and the unjust. But unless we accept the gospel, it won't be the good news for us. If we pass it off as a useless fairy tale, the coming reality will be horrible indeed!

ONE SLEEPING SICKNESS SURVIVOR ASKED DR. SACKS WHAT WAS THE SENSE OF HIS HAVING CONTINUED TO LIVE.

Several of those cut down by the sleeping sickness epidemic and suddenly awakened decades later by L-dopa experienced moments of insight that gave them only a heartrending sense of their enormous loss.

One despairing man named Rolando could not escape Parkinsonlike symptoms despite treatment with L-dopa. He told Dr. Sacks, "I've been shut up in different places with illness since the day I was born. Why couldn't I have died as a kid? What's the sense, what's the use, of my life here?"

The sad fact is, of course, that the victims of sleeping sickness did not individually bring this tragedy on themselves. The same is not true, however, for that other deadly slumber of sin. If we do not accept a cure for our separation from God, we will become responsible for the final tragedy.

The second coming of Christ slays the wicked living, and the wicked dead remain in their graves. All the followers of Christ go to heaven with Him. But what happens here on earth while the righteous reign with Christ for a thousand years?

Here is how John described it: "I saw an angel coming down out of heaven, having the key to the Abyss and holding in his hand a great chain. He seized the dragon, that ancient serpent, who is the devil, or Satan, and bound him for a thousand years" (Revelation 20:1, 2).

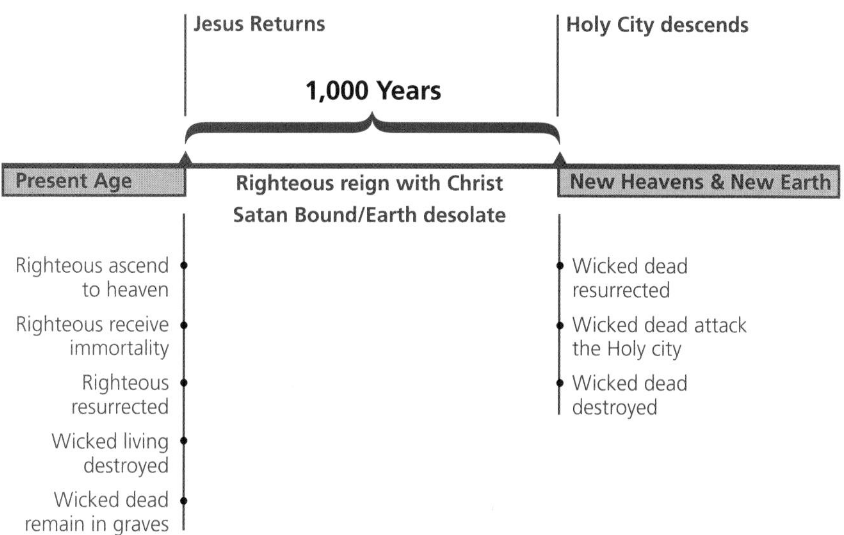

THE MILLENNIUM

Although the word does not appear in the Bible, scholars call this period the millennium. The word "millennium" comes from the Latin *mille*, 1,000, and *annum*, years—"1,000 years." During this time Satan will remain bound in a bottomless pit. But what does that mean?

The Greek word often translated "bottomless pit" is *abyssos*. We get our English word "abyss" from it. *Abyssos* refers to a very deep place—the depths, even the mythological underworld where the dead go. It describes a hole so deep that no one can find its bottom. In the Greek translation of the Old Testament called the Septuagint (usually abbreviated LXX), the word *abyssos* appears in the second verse of the Bible to describe the condition of Planet Earth prior to Creation week (Genesis 1:2) and is often translated simply "deep." This same passage expands what this "deep" was like, portraying it as "formless and empty" with darkness . . . over the surface of the deep *[abyssos]*."

Although the LXX rendering of Jeremiah 4:23-27 does not use the Greek word *abyssos*, it does use terminology directly from Genesis 1:2, depicting the future state of the earth as being "formless and empty." Here's what the prophet said of the devastation he saw in vision: "I looked at the

earth, and it was formless and empty; and at the heavens, and their light was gone. I looked at the mountains, and they were quaking; all the hills were swaying. I looked, and there were no people; every bird in the sky had flown away. I looked, and the fruitful land was a desert; all its towns lay in ruins before the Lord, before his fierce anger. This is what the Lord says: 'The whole land will be ruined, though I will not destroy it completely.'"

That's the way it will be on earth after the Second Coming. All human beings will be dead, and everything will be devastated. The utter destruction of sin will stare Satan in the face.

If Satan is alive throughout the 1,000 years, how is he "bound" (Revelation 20:2)? It's unlikely that a literal chain restricts him. Remember that Revelation is a book of symbols. John is depicting the earth to be a terrible prison for Satan. Thus the devil finds himself bound by a chain of circumstances and thrown into the abyss, the place where the deceased go. All the righteous have gone to heaven, and all the wicked are dead. In other words, Satan no longer has anyone to tempt, manipulate, or deceive.

> **"THE DEAD IN CHRIST WILL RISE FIRST. . . . WE WILL BE WITH THE LORD FOREVER."**

This earth will become like a bottomless pit for Satan. The wreckage of the planet clearly reveals that the wages of sin is death. And looking on, the whole universe will bear witness to the terrible truth of those words as he now confronts the horrible results of rebellion.

But what will the righteous be doing? According to Revelation 20:6 those who rose in the first resurrection will be priests of God and will reign with Him for 1,000 years.

Think about being with Christ during the millennium. It will be inexpressibly wonderful. But you'll also have a lot of questions. You may wonder why a loved one isn't there. Or you may not understand why a friend—who seemed like such a good person—didn't get saved. But our gracious God will answer all our questions. We'll be able to review God's decisions.

HARRY ANDERSON

Speaking of the redeemed during the millennium, John declares: "I saw thrones on which were seated those who had been given authority to judge" (Revelation 20:4).

JUDGING THE WICKED

We know that God is the ultimate judge. Only the all-knowing Lord can preside over the heavenly courts. But in some sense the redeemed will also participate in the divine judgment. Revelation 20:12 says that the "books were opened." The redeemed now in heaven will then be allowed to look over heaven's records, a kind of judicial review. Paul stated: "Do you not know that the saints will judge the world? . . . Do you not know that we will judge angels?" (1 Corinthians 6:2, 3).

We'll be looking over the cases of people who have chosen to be lost.

Paul wrote: "Therefore judge nothing before the appointed time; wait till the Lord comes. He will bring to light what is hidden in darkness and will expose the motives of men's hearts" (1 Corinthians 4:5). His statement implies that one day we will fully understand why it was impossible for God to save some people. We may not understand on our own why this person or that person didn't make it. But God can show us all the ways He tried to win a person, all that He did to enable love to break through. He can reveal what was really in people's hearts, things that they kept hidden so well in this life.

At the end of that period of judicial review we will fall at God's feet and proclaim that He is just and fair. The redeemed will sing: "Yes, Lord God Almighty, true and just are your judgments" (Revelation 16:7).

The millennium will answer all your questions—questions about other people, questions about your own life. You will come to understand completely why certain things happened and how everything ultimately fits into a wonderful plan.

Now let's look at what happens at the *end* of the millennium, the close of the 1,000 years. John wrote: "When the thousand years are over, Satan will be released from his prison and will go out to deceive the nations in the four corners of the earth" (Revelation 20:7, 8).

"But I thought the wicked were dead," I hear you saying. "Whom is Satan going to deceive?"

THE LAKE OF FIRE IS THE SECOND DEATH, IN WHICH THE WICKED CEASE TO EXIST FOREVER.

Let's look at the big picture. Another great event takes place at the end of the millennium—the second resurrection: "The rest of the dead did not come to life until the thousand years were ended" (verse 5). As we noted earlier, "the rest of the dead" are the wicked dead. We have a resurrection to life for believers at the beginning of the millennium and a resurrection to damnation for the wicked at the end of the millennium.

The apostle describes the scene: "The sea gave up the dead that were in it, and death and Hades gave up the dead that were in them, and each person was judged according to what he had done. Then death and Hades were thrown into the lake of fire. The lake of fire is the second death. If anyone's name was not found written in the book of life, he was thrown into the lake of fire" (verses 13-15).

Here we have the earth's final tragedy, an awakening that does not last, a rising from sleep that leads only to eternal slumber. It is difficult for

PHOTODISC

us to imagine the sense of loss of those who look at God in all His love and glory and realize that they will never enjoy life with Him in heaven. They will miss out on eternity. What inexpressible anguish that thought must bring! No wonder Scripture describes it as a time of weeping and gnashing of teeth.

It's almost impossible to conceive of such a sense of loss. But those victims of the sleeping sickness epidemic whom Dr. Sacks temporarily freed from their strange condition but who finally slipped back into unconsciousness—they give us some idea, some hint, of that terrible, final awakening. Those who discovered suddenly that they had plummeted from youth into dying old age, that all the years in between had disappeared without a trace—only they can tell us something of the final tragedy on this planet.

THE BEAUTY OF THE WORLD IS BUT A FAINT REFLECTION OF THE GLORY OF THE EARTH RESTORED.

But even more important events will take place at the end of the millennium.

PHOTODISC

God is going to remake the earth as it was in the Garden of Eden. "Then I saw a new heaven and a new earth," John said, "for the first heaven and the first earth had passed away. . . . I saw the Holy City, the New Jerusalem, coming down out of heaven from God, prepared as a

bride beautifully dressed for her husband" (Revelation 21:1, 2).

The revelator is here describing our return trip, after the millennium, from heaven back to earth. We will be in that New Jerusalem, a kind of celestial spaceship. And its destination—its destiny—is to reclaim Planet Earth.

"And I heard a loud voice from the throne saying, 'Now the dwelling of God is with men, and he will live with them. They will be his people, and God himself will be with them and be their God'" (verse 3). God will live with us in this New Jerusalem! He will transform our sin-scarred world into a spectacular footstool for His throne.

While for the redeemed it is wonderful news, that is not the case for Satan at that moment. Seeing the Holy City coming down, he responds in one last act of defiance and rebellion. He can't help himself.

Remember, God has resurrected the wicked from all ages. As Revelation 20:8 tells us, "in number they are like the sand on the seashore." Satan gathers them from all over the earth into one vast army. He will take as much time as necessary to build his forces under the brightest generals of all time and furnish them with the most sophisticated killing machines that great minds can devise. Then he attacks the Holy City. "They marched across the breadth of the earth and surrounded the camp of God's people, the city he loves" (verse 9).

Satan's last gasp, it's the last battle in the long conflict between him and Christ for the heart of the universe. And it's the final struggle of the war called Armageddon. The armies of hell rush toward the city from

GOD'S PURPOSES IN THE MILLENNIUM	
1	During the 1,000 years God reveals His love, justice, and mercy to the saved of all ages.
2	Each of the redeemed has the opportunity to look over the heavenly records to understand fully God's dealing in every life.
3	Angelic beings and the redeemed behold the devastation of the earth and see the ultimate results of sin. Echoing and reechoing throughout the universe are the words "The wages of sin is death" (Romans 6:23).
4	God demonstrates for a final time during the millennial period to the entire universe that His handling of the conflict between good and evil had as its motivation sacrificial love, with the sole desire of saving His people.
5	The universe now sees that the lost are finally destroyed because of their own choices.

heaven. "But fire came down from heaven and devoured them" (verse 9). That fire utterly consumes those outside the city. The ultimate fate of the wicked, it is what happens when people throw Christ off the throne in their lives. Before their annihilation they'll find themselves on the outside looking in.

The fire that destroys the wicked also cleanses the earth. It wipes away all the scars of sin and removes the ravages of rebellion. And that is how God makes all things new. Now He can create a new heaven and a new earth.

Let me tell you about another of those patients who received L-dopa and awakened from a long imprisoning slumber.

Growing up in the early 1900s, Magda was a happy child. She did well in high school, receiving honors both as a scholar and as an athlete. But in 1918, while working as a secretary, she contracted the sleeping sickness. Magda recovered after a few months, but in 1923 again started showing signs of the disease and slipped into a state of limbo that lasted 45 years. The woman spent her days in institutions sitting in a wheelchair, motionless, expressionless, apparently oblivious to anything happening around her. Those who provided nursing care regarded her as a hopeless case.

But when administered L-dopa, Magda gradually awakened. First she found her voice again; then she began writing a few sentences. Soon she was able to feed herself and walk a bit. And then a whole person blossomed, where there had been only a shell. Dr. Sacks wrote that Magda "showed an intelligence, a charm, and a humor, which had been almost totally concealed by her disease."

Happily recalling her childhood in Vienna, she talked nostalgically about school excursions and family holidays. But she did not remain trapped in the past. Somehow the courageous woman found the strength to cope with the 45-year gap in her life. Renewing emotional ties with her daughters and sons-in-law, she discovered her grandchildren and enjoyed visits with many other relatives who came to see the miracle of Magda restored to reality.

Such an incredible awakening is the hope that God offers to each of us even now, no matter how long or deep our slumber in sin has been. And when the kingdom of God shines down on our planet, we will joyfully ascend in the air with Jesus Christ.

We don't have to remain trapped in the tragedies of life in this sinful world—unable to bridge the unimaginable gap between life as we've known it and the life God wants to give us today. Nor do we have to remain numb in the grip of a deadening affliction called sin.

But when God resurrects the righteous it will be the opposite of the awakenings of Dr. Sacks' sleeping sickness patients. We won't wake up and suddenly find ourselves old. Instead, we will discover ourselves young again with new bodies, re-created like the glorious resurrected body of Christ. Those who labored with disabilities all their lives—paralysis, blindness, scars—will awake in perfect health.

Those who accept the good news about Jesus as the great Life-giver can look forward to that ultimate awakening.

CHAPTER 17

LIVING UNDER THE NEXT SUPERPOWER

John Godfrey Saxe, a nineteenth-century American lawyer, poet, and editor, once wrote a delightful poem about an old story allegedly from the country of India. He called it "The Blind Men and the Elephant." The poem tells about six blind men who came upon an elephant and tried to determine what such a creature was like just by touching it.

The first man, Saxe wrote, felt the elephant's side and concluded that the animal was like a wall. The first part of the elephant that the second man happened to grab was its tusk, so he maintained that an elephant had the characteristics of a spear. The third ran his hands around the elephant's squirming trunk and declared that an elephant resembled a snake. The fourth blind man totally disagreed, for he had reached his arms around the elephant's leg and was certain that an elephant was like a tree. The fifth man found the elephant's huge ear, so he told the others that clearly an elephant had the appearance of a fan. Finally, the sixth man discovered the elephant's swinging tail and shouted that the animal had the shape of a rope.

The six men, according to the poem, then began to argue loudly, growing increasingly angry with each other. Each man stubbornly thought that he was right, and none of them were about to give up their opinion.

After sharing the story of six blind men who angrily disagreed on what an elephant was, John Godfrey Saxe ended his poem with these words:

"And so these men of Indostan

LARS JUSTINEN

Disputed loud and long,
Each in his own opinion
Exceeding stiff and strong,
Though each was partly in the right,
And all were in the wrong!"

Then, in the final lines of the poem, poet Saxe let his readers in on the reason he wrote the poem. The six blind men, he made clear, illustrate how ill-advised and wrongheaded so many religious arguments are.

"So oft in theologic wars,
The disputants, I ween,
Rail on in utter ignorance
Of what each other mean,
And prate about an Elephant
Not one of them has seen!"

PHOTODISC

The poet acknowledged the unhappy truth that when it comes to their religious beliefs, people can be extremely passionate and stubbornly certain that they are right. Yet so often these same people are speaking from utter ignorance instead.

One such religious topic is the belief about heaven. Opinions about it vary wildly. What is heaven? Does it even exist? If so, where is it—and what is it like there?

IS HEAVEN REAL?

Many people believe that heaven is a wishful fantasy that weak-minded people cling to in order to cope with, or escape from, the tough realities of life here on earth. Some assume that eventually everybody will end up in heaven. But others say very few people will make it there. And nearly all arguments about heaven typically generate more heat than light—more controversy than understanding.

So much confusion! So many opinions! But why? Why all these different opinions and theories when the Bible itself is full of details about heaven? Yes, God wants us to know what heaven is like so that we will want to be there! Heaven is not a place He is trying to keep secret from us.

According to a Harris poll taken in January of 2003, 82 percent of Americans believe that a heaven does exist. But the truth is that these days most people—and that includes many Christians, too—spend very little time thinking about heaven. From the moment we wake up in the morning till we collapse in exhaustion into our beds again at night, we're running, going, doing—we're eating, working, sitting in classes or committees, shopping, cleaning house, fixing cars, paying bills, and rushing to appointments. We find our days filled with relating to other people—family members, coworkers, strangers, neighbors, clerks and salespeople, and the voices of unseen people who contact us by phone or e-mail.

Behind it all is the endless din of the daily news of what's happening in our world: the wars, the scandals, the disasters, the violence, the ebb and flow of human politics and power and passion. Competing also for our attention—and perhaps with almost too much success—are the not-quite-real worlds of sports and entertainment.

> MOST PEOPLE HAVE A BORING CONCEPT ABOUT WHAT HEAVEN WILL BE LIKE.

Meanwhile we Christians believe that somewhere inconceivably far away in the universe is an unseen place that we've been taught about, and it's called heaven. It's part of the distant future, not the here and now. And though we can see and touch the immediate environment we live in every day, heaven is out of sight and out of reach. Therefore, it hardly seems real. Besides, our lives move so fast and are so full that we can barely keep pace with what's happening right around us, much less stop to contemplate a place to which we've never been.

Part of the problem, too, is that what many of us typically believe about heaven leaves us considerably less than impressed. What if, for example, you're just not really into playing harps all day? What if fleecy

PHOTODISC

THE WONDERS OF EVEN THIS SIN-DAMAGED WORLD MAKE THE IDEA OF FLOATING ON CLOUDS DISAPPOINTING.

white clouds and halos and singing in the heavenly choir leaves you cold? And do you really have to run around in a long white robe all the time?

Undoubtedly one reason so many of us have a hard time getting excited about eternity is that we carry around a stunted and juvenile view of heaven as a spectacular setting in which we float around endlessly doing bland things and "being holy." Sort of like spending a vacation on a breathtaking tropical beach while reading the phone book.

Many of us will live 70, 80, or 90 years in this world. Some of us may even reach 100. Yet even then life races by at blinding speed. Just as we seem to be getting started, it's over. This world is so very temporary. But heaven, which the Bible says will ultimately move to a new, re-created earth, is our real and final home. There we'll spend hundreds, thousands, millions, and billions upon trillions of years in an endless eternity. So maybe it behooves us to do a little thinking about the place we will spend the rest of our lives.

While John the revelator was exiled on the little island of Patmos off the coast of Turkey, God showed him His city in vision: "I saw a new heaven and a new earth, for the first heaven and the first earth had passed away, and there was no longer any sea. I saw the Holy City, the new Jerusalem, coming down out of heaven from God, prepared as a bride beautifully dressed for her husband" (Revelation 21:1, 2). Few illustrations depict happiness and beauty better than that of a bride preparing for her wedding day.

This city is not just something that John saw and knew about—God's people have been aware of it throughout the ages. God tells us that all of His holy prophets had spoken about God's plan to deal with a sin-damaged world. Peter told the people of old Jerusalem that God would "send the Christ, who has been appointed for you—even Jesus. He must remain in heaven until the time comes for God to restore everything, as he promised long ago through his holy prophets" (Acts 3:20, 21).

A RESTORED WORLD

What is God going to restore? What Adam and Eve lost—paradise on Planet Earth, an earth made new! This old world, contaminated by pollutants, needing fresh water and pure air, and filled with violence and suffering, wouldn't be much of a gift. But God is going to give us a new earth—a perfect world populated by redeemed people. It will be just like the earth was when the Lord created Adam and Eve.

When Eve listened to the temptations of the serpent and disobeyed God, she in turn gave the forbidden fruit to Adam, and he also ate. Sadly, they turned over their dominion of this earth to God's enemy. They lost everything. The Lord had no choice but to drive them from their home in Eden. God put cherubim to guard the gate so that Adam and Eve would not eat fruit from the tree of life.

As people multiplied on the earth, sin also increased, until the majority did not know or worship the Creator. In fact, from the time the Tower of Babel was constructed, almost all the people on earth had forgotten their God and His promises. But one family in Ur of the Chaldees—Abraham and his relatives—still worshipped the true God. The Lord

PHOTODISC

promised Abraham that his seed, or descendants, would inherit the earth and would see the restitution of all that Adam and Eve had lost.

Abraham accepted by faith that God would fulfill His promises. Yet the patriarch lived here on this earth as a stranger or pilgrim. As Paul wrote, "he was looking forward to the city with foundations, whose architect and builder is God" (Hebrews 11:10). This same city, which the ancient patriarchs longed for, still waits for the moment when faith becomes sight.

SCRIPTURE PROMISES A WORLD IN WHICH THE WOLF WILL NO LONGER BE A PREDATOR AND IT AND THE LAMB CAN LIE DOWN IN PEACE.

Marco Polo, the Italian explorer, returned home from China after 24 years in eastern Asia. He told such incredible tales that his friends thought he had gone mad. For example, he said he had traveled to a city full of silver and gold. He had seen black stones that burned (Marco Polo wasn't familiar with coal) and cloth that refused to catch fire even when thrown into the flames. (No one had ever heard of asbestos.) Furthermore, he spoke of huge serpents 10 paces long with jaws wide enough to swallow a man (Europeans had never seen a crocodile) and of nuts the size of a person's head (they had never seen coconuts).

The people just laughed at such stories. Years later, when Marco was dying, a devout priest at his bedside urged the explorer to recant all the tall tales he'd told. The explorer refused. "I do not tell half of what I saw, because no one would have believed me."

Words were not adequate to express the

beauties the writers of the Bible have told us about the new earth and the Holy City. As Marco Polo said, "I do not tell half of what I saw." The prophet Isaiah back in the Old Testament wrote: "Since ancient times no one has heard, no ear has perceived, no eye has seen any God besides you, who acts on behalf of those who wait for him" (Isaiah 64:4).

HARRY ANDERSON

THE HEAVENLY CITY

Through God's Holy Spirit His prophets could share with us some of the beauties of the new earth and the Holy City, the New Jerusalem.

The book of Revelation gives us a breathtaking description of the Holy City that will be the dazzling home of the redeemed. "The wall of the city had twelve foundations, and on them were the names of the twelve apostles of the Lamb. . . . The foundations of the city walls were decorated with every kind of precious stone" (Revelation 21:14-19). The apostle also specified the size of the New Jerusalem: "The city was laid out like a square, as long as it was wide. He measured the city with the rod and found it to be 12,000 stadia [about 1,400 miles] in length, and as wide and high as it is long" (verse 16). Furthermore, "the twelve gates were

Harry Anderson

twelve pearls. . . . The great street of the city was of pure gold, like transparent glass" (verse 21).

If a city like that existed anywhere on earth today, believe me, everyone would be packing up to move there regardless of the cost!

Instead of floating among the clouds, the redeemed will find themselves on solid earth. But it will be a new earth—that's what we have to look forward to. Earth II will be a Garden of Eden restored. The prophet Isaiah gives us a glimpse of the kind of things the Lord has in store for us: "The desert and the parched land will be glad; the wilderness will rejoice and blossom" (Isaiah 35:1).

GOD WILL WIPE AWAY EVERY TEAR FROM THE EYES OF THE REDEEMED.

This promised world is a haven in which pain won't exist. It will have no cancer, no heart attacks, no arthritis, no fevers, no illness—forever! Here's another glimpse from Isaiah: "No one living in Zion will say, 'I am ill'" (Isaiah 33:24). "Then will the lame leap like a deer, and the mute tongue shout for joy. Water will gush forth in the wilderness and streams in the desert" (Isaiah 35:6).

The book of Revelation echoes this same wonderful picture as it assures us what life in the New Jerusalem will be like: "He will wipe away every tear from their eyes. There will be no more death or mourning or crying or pain, for the old order of things has passed away" (Revelation 21:4). The redeemed will no longer have to cope with sorrow and death. They can love others without the constant fear of losing them. Heaven will have no funerals or cemeteries. The inhabitants of God's new world will have nothing to fear. "No longer will violence be heard in your land, nor ruin or destruction within your borders" (Isaiah 60:18). Just peace, harmony, and love.

In the New Jerusalem our relentless search for a fountain of youth will, at last, find its fulfillment. "Then the angel showed me the river of the water of life, as clear as crystal, flowing from the throne of God and of the Lamb down the middle of the great street of the city. On each side

THE SEVEN MOST IMPORTANT BIBLE TRUTHS ABOUT HEAVEN

1	Heaven is a real place, not some make-believe fairy tale or figment of a mystic's imagination (John 14:1-3; 2 Peter 3:13; Isaiah 65:17).
2	Heaven is a place for people with real, glorious, immortal bodies (1 Corinthians 15:51-54; 1 Thessalonians 4:16, 17).
3	Heaven is a place for real activities (Isaiah 65:21-23).
4	Heaven is a place of real fellowship with the greatest minds of the ages (Matthew 8:11).
5	Heaven is a place of lasting peace, genuine satisfaction, and eternal happiness (Isaiah 65:25; Revelation 21:3, 4).
6	Heaven is a place of exhilarating worship and overflowing praise to the God who made us and redeemed us (Revelation 4:11; 5:11, 12; Isaiah 66:22, 23).
7	Heaven is a place of eternal fellowship with our Lord (Revelation 21:1-4; 22:1-5).

of the river stood the tree of life, bearing twelve crops of fruit, yielding its fruit every month. And the leaves of the tree are for the healing of the nations" (Revelation 22:1, 2). The river of life is the fountain of youth. We'll enjoy perfect bodies with boundless energy to explore the wonders about us.

Even in the closest of our relationships in this life we experience tension and disagreement and misunderstandings. Many suffer from verbal, physical, and emotional abuse. Divorce and alienation are rampant. But in heaven we will live in perfect harmony with everyone. We will have no unmet needs for intimacy and communication and affirmation. All our relationships will work perfectly and bring us deep, lasting, profound joy. Imagine all that you've ever wanted or hoped for in love or friendship—it's yours forever.

Heaven will be a place permanently without disappointment, disillusionment, discouragement, depression, debt, and divorce. Nor will we have to fight any more spiritual battles; we can simply enjoy spiritual growth and personal communion with God. Boredom will never be a problem. We will be able to travel anywhere in the universe at will. Picking out some area of knowledge, we will be able to learn everything possible about it. Or we can choose any skill and develop it as far as we desire.

Our hands, designed by God to work out the visions of our minds, will build and create freely. We'll be able to produce anything we can think of! And our energy will be renewed from week to week. Further, Isaiah tells us: "'From one Sabbath to another, all mankind will come and bow down before me, says the Lord" (Isaiah 66:23). We'll have wonderful worship and communion with our Creator. The Sabbath celebration even now brings us new life and vision to our marred old earth. But it will energize us in an even more wonderful way amid the splendors of heaven. Our sense of community, our experience of praise—all will exceed anything we've witnessed here below.

CAPITAL OF THE UNIVERSE

Even more amazing, God has promised that one day our world will be the capital of His universe! "And I heard a loud voice from the throne saying, 'Now the dwelling of God is with men, and he will live with them. They will be his people, and God himself will be with them and be their God'" (Revelation 21:3). "They will see his face" (Revelation 22:4).

Imagine standing in His immediate presence and looking directly into His eyes as He fixes His gaze on you. There you will see Him looking gently back at you, eyes filled with love that words alone can never describe. They are the eyes of the One who dreamed of you in His mind, then called you into existence. They are the eyes of the One who filled your lungs with your first breath and every breath that followed. They are the eyes of the One whose power keeps your heart constantly beating.

Those eyes once closed in death for you so that you might share this moment in heaven with Him. They are full of perfect, unconditional, all-encompassing eternal love. As you look into those eyes you realize that finally your pain and your loss and your sin and your separation and your fear are all gone and that you are perfectly loved and accepted in this moment—and will be so for all eternity.

Yes, nothing will ever match the all-consuming joy of gazing into the face of your Creator and feeling such overpowering gratitude as you never dreamed possible—of realizing that because of Him your heart will never be empty, your brow will never be furrowed, your body never weary, your soul never lacking.

As you stand there immersed in acceptance and approval and unconditional love, those eyes brighten as He smiles at you. His total attention in this moment is focused on you and you alone. Lost in those smiling eyes, you suddenly realize that heaven is much more than gold streets and a glassy sea. It's basking in the presence of Someone who loves you more than His own life—and knowing that you have all eternity to find out just how much and why.

Quite some years ago a young medical doctor and his wife, living in southern California, longed to have children. But years passed, and it didn't happen—so they decided to adopt a little boy. However, some time later the wife also gave birth to a baby boy. They were overjoyed. Now their family was complete.

A few years later the doctor came home for lunch, dropping his black bag by the front door. As he and his wife ate, the boys saw the bag and decided to play doctor.

When the physician started to leave for his office, he noticed his bag had been opened. Terror struck his heart at the sight inside. A bottle of lethal pills lay open, some of them scattered on the rug. He called to the boys and asked if they had swallowed any of the pills. The older boy, trying to protect the little fellow, said, "Yes, I did."

Immediately the parents rushed him to the hospital and had his stomach pumped. The doctor and his wife went home, relieved that their son was all right. But when they arrived home, their other little son was dead. Their grief was beyond expression.

The next week the mother, in a broken voice, related the story during a prayer meeting at their church. With tears streaming down her cheeks, she ended by saying, "I'm homesick for heaven—I feel I cannot wait."

That phrase lingered in the mind of the pastor, Henry de Fluiter. In time he wrote a song by that title—"Homesick for Heaven."

Are you homesick for heaven? Have you had enough of the tears and trials of life here on earth—and you're ever so ready to go home? Are you weary of the battle against your own selfish nature—exhausted by the unceasing drumbeat of tragic, violent, and depressing news every time you watch TV or read a newspaper? Do you long to be reunited with loved ones whom death has taken from you?

INVITATION TO ETERNITY

If so, please know that immediately after describing our eternal heavenly home, God ends the book of Revelation—and the Bible itself—with this invitation: "The Spirit and the bride say, 'Come!' And let him who hears say, 'Come!' Whoever is thirsty, let him come; and whoever wishes, let him take the free gift of the water of life" (Revelation 22:17).

HARRY ANDERSON

The final words of the last book of the Bible are our Lord's loving invitation to be with Him forever in heaven. Heaven is too good to miss. It is too wonderful to lose out on. Have you made your personal decision to commit your life to this Jesus, who wants to spend all eternity with you?

Opening your heart to Him, have you told Him that you are willing to do whatever He asks? that you are willing to follow His truth wherever it leads? Why not bow your head right now and in your own words thank Him for His love, His forgiveness, His power, and His truth? Become a citizen of history's last and eternal superpower.

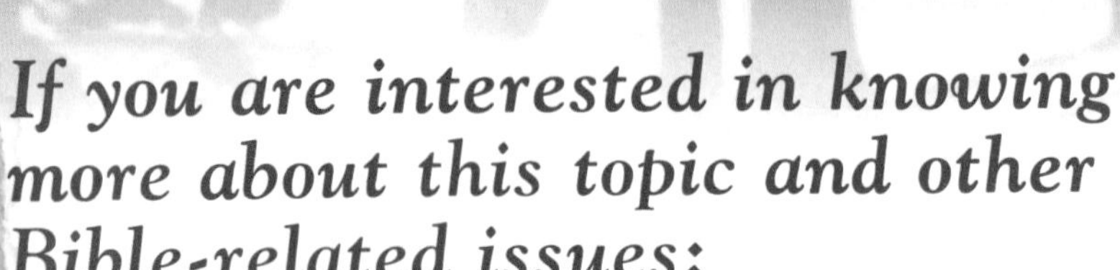

If you are interested in knowing more about this topic and other Bible-related issues:

- Visit **www.itiswritten.com** to view a weekly Bible study program online and use the free online Bible studies.

- Find answers to hundreds of Bible questions in 16 languages at **www.Bibleinfo.com.**

- Explore Bible lessons, games, and stories just for kids at **www.KidsBibleinfo.com.**

- Study the Bible systematically with study guides or with a Bible study group. Call
1-800-HIS-WORD (1-800-447-9673)
or leave a message at www.800HISWORD.com.

- Find more books on Bible-related topics at **www.reviewandherald.org.**

- Request Bible study guides by mail. Send your name and address to:

DISCOVER
It Is Written
Box 0
Thousand Oaks, CA 91359